150 Best New Apartment Ideas

150 Best New Apartment Ideas

HARPER
DESIGN
An Imprint of HarperCollins Publishers

HarperCollins books may be purchased for educational, business, or sales promotional use.
For information, please write: Special Markets Department, HarperCollins*Publishers*,
10 East 53rd Street, New York, NY 10022.

First published in 2011 by:
Harper Design
An Imprint of HarperCollins*Publishers*
10 East 53rd Street
New York, NY 10022
Tel.: (212) 207-7000
Fax: (212) 207-7654
harperdesign@harpercollins.com
www.harpercollins.com

Distributed throughout the world by:
HarperCollins*Publishers*
10 East 53rdStreet
New York, NY 10022
Fax: (212) 207-7654

Editorial coordinator: Simone K. Schleifer
Assistant to editorial coordination: Aitana Lleonart
Editor and text: Francesc Zamora Mola
Art director: Mireia Casanovas Soley
Design and layout coordination: Claudia Martínez Alonso
Layout: Guillermo Pfaff Puigmartí
Cover layout: María Eugenia Castell

ISBN: 978-0-06-206723-4

Library of Congress Control Number: 2010928178

Printed in Spain

CONTENTS

Introduction

Making your living space a comfortable place you want to be at all times is not an easy task and can even be intimidating when you don't know how to go about doing it. The truth is that it takes time, patience, and a big stack of home decorating magazines to achieve satisfying results. Decorating is all about personal taste and expressing yourself through creative ideas to produce an environment that reflects your personality. Whether you have recently moved to an empty apartment or are redecorating, there are ways to give your apartment a new look with a personalized flair. You will find that not only are there a gazillion options, but also you can change the decoration of your apartment or parts of it at any time with new, trendy ideas.

While an expert's advice always comes in handy, there are certain aspects you should handle yourself before undertaking your decorating project: First, define the area you want to decorate, and be specific about your needs by drafting a wish list. Second, establish a budget and prioritize your purchases and tasks. Third, decide on a theme to focus on when selecting colors, furniture, and accessories. Your decorator can take it from there, or you can venture out on your own, finding inspiration in magazines, books and catalogs, online blogs, and shops. No matter how tedious the process may be, especially in the early stages, you will see things slowly start falling into place, and the experience will eventually prove exciting and, most important, gratifying.

Sleek and Modern

The open informality of a 1920s industrial loft is overlaid with a sumptuous program for living, entertaining, and the display of contemporary art. The open plan benefits from northern and southern light exposures, making the central living area a naturally and theatrically lit courtyard.

Chelsea Loft Residence

Architect: Gabellini Sheppard Associates
Location: New York, NY, USA
Year of construction: 2007
Photography: Paul Warchol Photography

The surrounding private spaces—
bedrooms, bathrooms, storage, and
service areas—rise on a natural-finish
Brazilian walnut plinth.

Floor plan

1. Kitchen
2. Dining room
3. Sitting area
4. Living room
5. Master bathroom
6. Master bedroom
7. Bedroom
8. Bathroom

001

Between the articulated ceiling beams, ambient light coves combine with focused gallery lighting to enable a variety of atmospheric states.

The two guest bedrooms, enclosed .
in matte translucent glass panels, are
positioned along the gallery that wraps
around the main living space.

The gut renovation of a loft with windows on only one exposure presented unique challenges specific to the space and to the art collector client. The project resulted in a fluid space that allows daylight into specific areas and maximizes wall space for large paintings and photographs.

Spring Street Loft

Architect: EOA | Elmslie Osler Architect
Location: New York, NY, USA
Year of construction: 2010
Photography: EOA | Elmslie Osler Architect

A blackened steel wall swings open to grant access to a freight elevator and serves as support for a large format art piece.

Floor plan

1. Entry
2. Hallway
3. Guest bedroom
4. Office
5. Bathroom
6. Kitchen
7. Closet
8. Master bathroom
9. Master bedroom
10. Living room

002

To make a large sliding door visually interesting, paint it with a daring combination of color.

The entry is clad in a reclaimed Brazilian barn wood that extends throughout the house to counterbalance the rigor of the steel and glass.

003

Install translucent glass doors and panels to bring natural light into dark rooms without compromising privacy.

Loft Hamburg

Architect: GRAFT Gesellschaft
von Architekten
Location: Hamburg, Germany
Year of construction: 2009
Photography: GRAFT
Gesellschaft von Architekten

This loft makes optimum use of an existing space with a freestanding walnut wood–clad core that contains a kitchen, a half bath, storage, and the supply of gas, electric, and water. The new space is thoughtfully designed to accommodate media and work requirements as well as living and lounging needs.

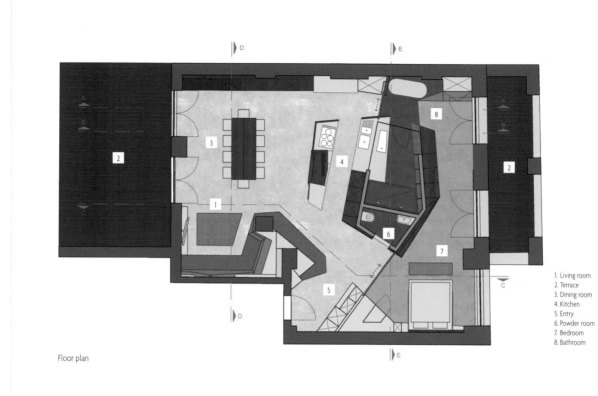

Floor plan

1. Living room
2. Terrace
3. Dining room
4. Kitchen
5. Entry
6. Powder room
7. Bedroom
8. Bathroom

The shape of the core offers interesting perspectives of the loft, which can be divided into separate sections by floor-to-ceiling sliding doors.

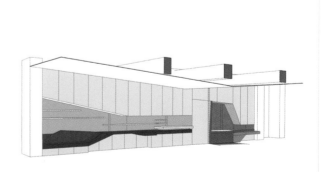

Service wall north

Wall panels and consoles that conceal media and work equipment combine with comfortable built-in banquettes to make the most of the space.

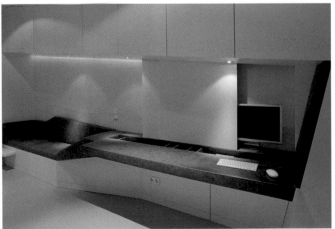

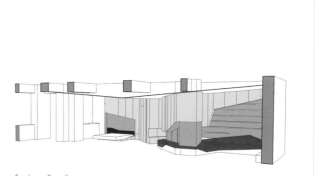

Service wall south

The built-in seating and equipment along the perimeter of the loft and the various cut-outs in the wood core seem to be carved out.

Recessed and cove lighting reinforce the dynamic design of the loft and enhance the subtlety of the finishes used on the different surfaces.

004

Stone veneer offers many advantages over natural stone: It comes in many sizes and is much lighter and easier to use than natural stone.

Materials such as stone and wood bring warmth to the loft. In the bathroom, stone serves as a backsplash that blends into the kitchen flooring.

Bathroom and kitchen floor plan and section

005

Natural stone adds character to interior walls and floors, but the application of a stone sealer is required to prevent soiling and staining.

Located atop a concrete high-rise, the original four-bedroom/four-bath penthouse was a rabbit's warren of confusing rooms. The program consisted in opening up the apartment to the views that the location offered, and addressing an environmental responsibility to alter the spaces as little as possible.

Ludwig Penthouse

Architect: Craig Steely Architecture
Location: San Francisco, CA, USA
Year of construction: 2009
Photography: Tim Griffith

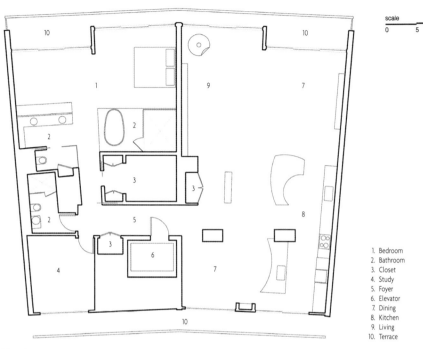

scale

0   5   10

N

1. Bedroom
2. Bathroom
3. Closet
4. Study
5. Foyer
6. Elevator
7. Dining
8. Kitchen
9. Living
10. Terrace

Floor plan

006

Don't limit yourself to the display of art pieces as a way to create focal areas. Pick one wall and use a special finish to turn it into art itself.

The elevator delivers directly into the apartment's foyer, whose wall is covered by a floor-to-ceiling mosaic of hand-cut glass.

007

When considering new wood cabinets, factors such as durability, cost, and appearance must be taken into account before making a final decision.

A floating mirrored divider and walls of acid-etched glass in varying opacities create privacy in the master bedroom and bathroom.

Carr Apartment

This simple program allowed for a focus on experimentation. This apartment is a mixture of reflections and texture: walls, doors, and cabinetry of figured koa and Macassar ebony, the brindle brown of the carpet, thick walls of etched and back-painted glass, and stainless steel counters.

Architect: Craig Steely Architecture
Location: San Francisco, CA, USA
Year of construction: 2009
Photography: Rien van Rijthoven

The inspiration for the floor-to-ceiling LED light installation came from the mood set by 1970s space-rock and ambient music.

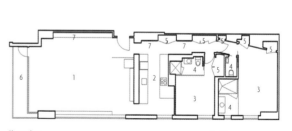

Floor plan

1. Living
2. Kitchen
3. Bedroom
4. Bathroom
5. Storage
6. Deck
7. Light wall

008

The industrial look of stainless steel can be lessened by using wood with an attractive grain and a warm glow on other surfaces.

The architect chose all the furniture as
well as the art, emphasizing a sort of
soothing, calm, yet spatial limbo.

Russian Hill High-Rise

This high-rise apartment is a sophisticated urban retreat designed to accentuate the owner's extensive art collection and the breathtaking views offered by the location. Programmatically, the main rooms are placed on the perimeter to access views and light, while an inner "cube" contains services and entertainment equipment.

Architect: Zack | de Vito
Architecture
Location: San Francisco, CA, USA
Year of construction: 2009
Photography: Bruce Damonte
Photography

009

The kitchen, storage, and bathrooms, which are grouped in the center of the apartment, allow for the surrounding space to be free of obstructive partitions.

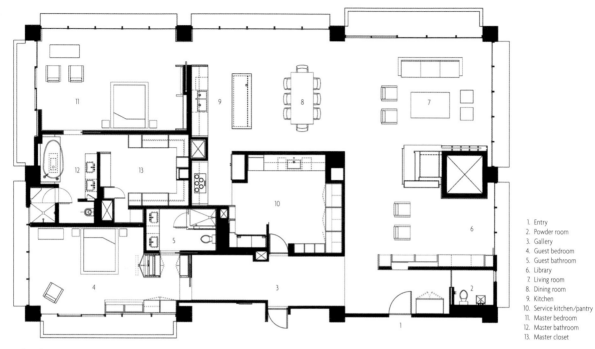

Floor plan

1. Entry
2. Powder room
3. Gallery
4. Guest bedroom
5. Guest bathroom
6. Library
7. Living room
8. Dining room
9. Kitchen
10. Service kitchen/pantry
11. Master bedroom
12. Master bathroom
13. Master closet

010

Light and humidity can damage art. Make sure all artwork is appropriately framed. Porous objects will need a coat of polyurethane.

011

Limited and repeating materials and colors define and clarify spaces and delineate transitions.

Market Street Penthouse

The duplex is subdivided into two living strips parallel to a window wall. A darker inner band, lined with natural materials, defines the entry, staircase, and pool/guest room on the second floor. A bright outer zone, lit by windows, defines the double-height living room, the kitchen/dining room, and the master bedroom suite on the second floor.

Architect: Joel Sanders Architect
Location: San Francisco, CA, USA
Year of construction: 2009
Photography: Rien van Rijthoven

Concrete, fritted glass, and stainless and powder-coated steel focus attention on the "sky zone" that frames city views.

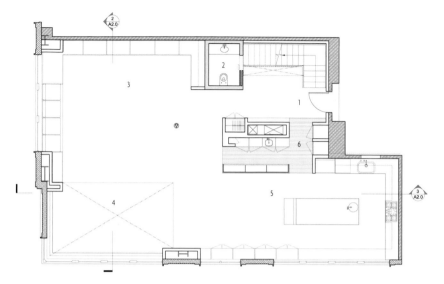

Lower level floor plan

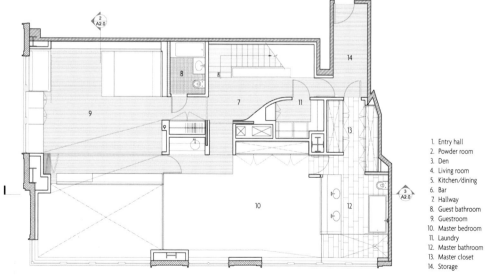

Upper level floor plan

1. Entry hall
2. Powder room
3. Den
4. Living room
5. Kitchen/dining
6. Bar
7. Hallway
8. Guest bathroom
9. Guestroom
10. Master bedroom
11. Laundry
12. Master bathroom
13. Master closet
14. Storage

The design strategy unifies the openings within a "sky zone," a recessed slot painted gray/blue that wraps the perimeter of the apartment.

In contrast with the "sky zone", a darker
inner band is lined with walnut paneling
defining the entry and the stairwell.

Architect: Siris / Coombs
Architects
Location: New York, NY, USA
Year of construction: 2009
Photography: Durston Saylor

The project combines two deteriorated penthouse apartments and transforms them into an airy rooftop residence with views over the Hudson River. A sequence of steel casement windows, which spans the entire east/west length of the building, creates an elegant connection between the two apartments.

Acoya Residence

This modern and unique home benefits from spacious rooms, which are subdivided into different activity areas to create dynamic and functional spaces. Light—both natural and artificial—is key to the design. It takes center stage with the use of backlit and translucent materials such as glass and onyx.

Architect: Pepe Calderin Design
Location: Miami Beach, FL, USA
Year of construction: 2008
Photography: Barry Grossman

Taking advantage of the large expanse of glass walls, all seating arrangements and spaces were designed to optimize the ocean views.

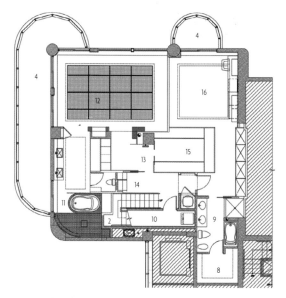

Lower level floor plan

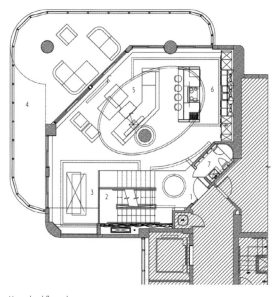

Upper level floor plan

1. Foyer
2. Stair
3. Dining room
4. Balcony
5. Living room
6. Kitchen

7. Powder room
8. Closet
9. Bathroom
10. Laundry
11. Master bathroom
12. Master bedroom

13. Vestibule
14. Stair hall
15. Dressing room
16. Bedroom

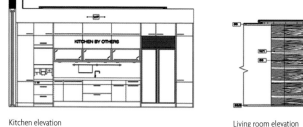

Kitchen elevation

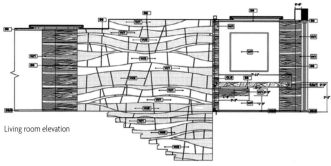

Living room elevation

Portofino Residence

This apartment consists of a large open public space that includes common areas. The living room, dining room, family room, and breakfast room are well-defined by the materials used on the floor and ceiling, by the difference in floor levels, and by the column lines.

Architect: Pascal Arquitectos
Location: Mexico DF, Mexico
Year of construction: 2008
Photography: Sófocles
Hernández

Floor plan

1. Vestibule
2. Toilet
3. Master walk-in closet
4. Master bathroom
5. Master bedroom
6. Bedroom
7. Bathroom
8. Walk-in closet
9. Breakfast nook
10. Living room
11. Dining room
12. Family room
13. Maid's room
14. Laundry room
15. Pantry
16. Kitchen

013

Explore options other than ceiling medallions to create a key feature that will help tie the ceiling into your home's design theme.

One of the apartment's main design features a long cabinet with a grid of glass doors along one wall that frames the dining room and the sitting area.

A large curved wall breaks the spatial rigidity generated by the column grid in the apartment and the building's octagonal footprint.

Penthouse at the Metropole

Architect: FORMA Design
Location: Washington, DC, USA
Year of construction: 2010
Photography: Geoffrey Hodgdon

Functionality dominates throughout this duplex, which has custom-designed cabinetry in the living areas, kitchen, and study. While wall space was required for the display of the clients' art collection, the apartment is open to the abundant natural light through the two-story atrium, which is equipped with shades.

In the kitchen, the pantry door is concealed behind a matching panel of quarter-sawed oak wood to create a streamlined look.

On the second floor, the original plan, which included two bedrooms, is altered to create a suite that comprises a sleeping area and an office.

U Loft

A U-shaped cabinet is inserted into a T-shaped loft, disembodying the space from its pre-existing structure and enclosure and creating a prolonged cross-graining of interior and "exterior" spaces.

Architect: Ten to One / Garrick Jones
Location: New York, NY, USA
Year of construction: 2008
Photography: Garrick Jones

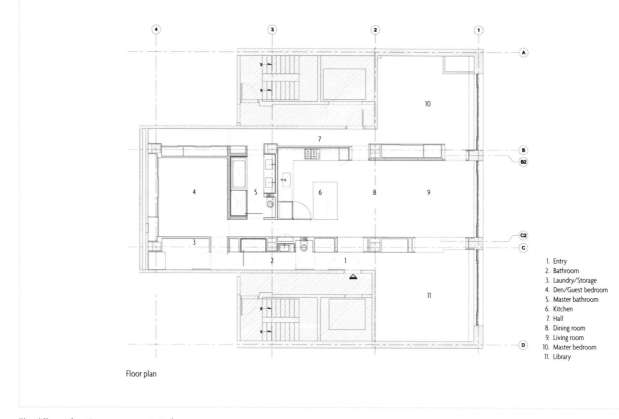

Floor plan

1. Entry
2. Bathroom
3. Laundry/Storage
4. Den/Guest bedroom
5. Master bathroom
6. Kitchen
7. Hall
8. Dining room
9. Living room
10. Master bedroom
11. Library

The different functions are concentrated
in the center of the apartment to
optimize the use of the space along the
wall with windows.

015

Adding a transom window to a solid wall or above a door in a hallway, bathroom, or dimly lit room can make the space feel less confined.

016

Also, walls short of the ceiling convey a feeling of airiness and allow for creative articulation, by exposing existing structures for example.

The designer recovered the historical memory of this early nineteenth-century apartment that had been obscured for many years by the previous remodels. Exposing the original wood floors, wood carpentry, iron radiators, period moldings, and high ceiling of the apartment was the priority.

Home in Madrid

Architect: Nacho Polo Interior Designer
Location: Madrid, Spain
Year of construction: 2007
Photography: Antonio Terron and Andrea Savini

Floor plan

1. Living/dining
2. Entry hall
3. Kitchen
4. Guest bedroom
5. Master bathroom
6. Master bedroom/dressing room
7. Bathroom

The original plan presented multiple small rooms. Some partitions were demolished to obtain larger rooms.

New and bright spaces were also achieved by recuperating windows that had been covered.

017

Give a little zest to a long and narrow hallway. Turn it into a gallery or a library if the width allows. Good lighting in this case is a must.

018

Removed from their original
context, antiques can provide
a baroque counterpoint to a
minimalist room.

For this three-bedroom apartment, the designer—and also owner—has created a contemporary space with a strong retro influence. He mixes custom-designed wooden furniture with classic designer pieces. The walls are in neutral grays, with furniture and decor providing strong accents of color.

Architect: **Hot Dog Decor**
Location: **Shanghai, China**
Year of construction: **2005**
Photography: **Peter Lam / Hot Dog Decor**

019

It is important to stick to a color theme when mixing old and new furniture to avoid making the space look too fragmented and disarranged.

Vintage furniture and decorations such as trunks and Venetian mirrors collected during the owner's world travels are mixed with designer pieces.

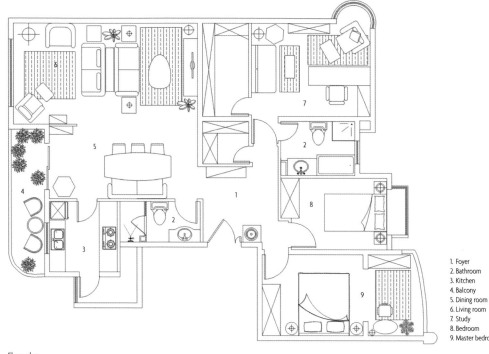

Floor plan

1. Foyer
2. Bathroom
3. Kitchen
4. Balcony
5. Dining room
6. Living room
7. Study
8. Bedroom
9. Master bedroom

020

It is not enough for a space
to simply look nice. It is more
important that a home reflect
the owner's personality.

Formal Unity

Architect: Guillermo Arias and
Luis Cuartas
Location: Bogotá, Colombia
Year of construction: 2005
Photography: Eduardo
Consuegra, Pablo Rojas, Álvaro
Gutiérrez

This loft occupies a large part of what was once a traditional residence in this 1930s-style building made up of several small rooms. Structurally, it was possible to clear the space in order to create one single room of ample proportions where the main area is organized around the double-sided fireplace.

The headboard acts as a valuable source
of natural light and leads to a small
interior patio that allows for ventilation.

Christian House

For this house, the architects remodeled an existing attic space of limited dimensions and constructed a new terrace on top of the attic. All the furniture was folded away behind the perimeter walls. The furniture is pulled out only when needed, leaving the center of the small space clear.

Architect: Barbara Appolloni
Location: Barcelona, Spain
Year of construction: 2009
Photography: Christian Schallert

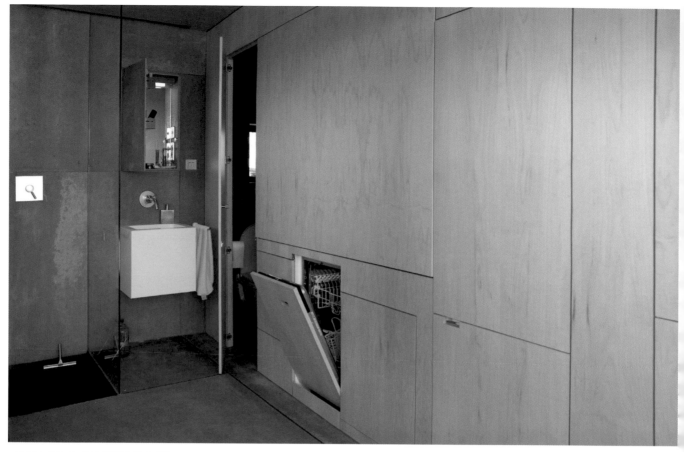

022

Multifunctional pieces of furniture, such as foldaway beds and folding tables and chairs, make the most of reduced spaces.

The bed folds under the floor of the existing terrace. It also serves as a bench, storage, and step.

To comfortably enjoy the views of the city, an Ipe wood deck with a large daybed and a tub were built on the terrace.

Notting Hill 2 Apartment

Located in the upper part of a converted church, this space was turned into a penthouse apartment. Planned as one single room with floor-to-ceiling windows, it occupies a corner of the building. The sleeping area can be closed off by means of translucent sliding panels.

Architect: Jonathan Clark
Architects
Location: London, UK
Year of construction: 2005
Photography: Jonathan Clark

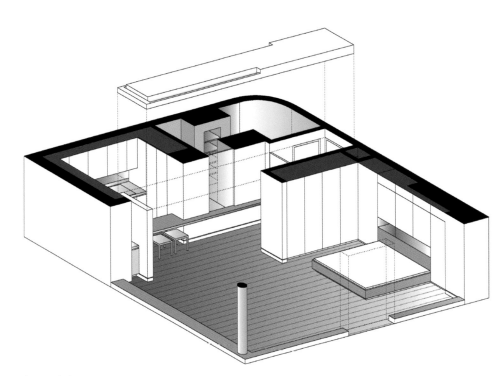

Axonometric view

023

In rooms with low ceilings, floating ceiling rafters and raised coffers with recessed lighting provide a greater sense of volume and height.

Electronically controlled wraparound curtains provide privacy as needed, changing the atmosphere of the place dramatically.

Floor plan

1. Living/dining
2. Bedroom
3. Bathroom
4. Kitchen

024

To bring light into a dark room, consider opening a hole in a wall and installing transparent or translucent glass.

Connor Residence

Architect: Emilio Fuscaldo,
Imogen Pullar / Nest Architects
Location: Elwood, Australia
Year of construction: 2009
Photography: Jesse Marlow

The design concept for this home was to create a series of new features and insert them into the existing space. This strategy does not interfere with the apartment's original art deco design but enhances it. These features consist of wood furniture pieces that instill a sense of simplicity and luxury.

025

Create harmony between adjacent rooms in the house by using some of the same materials and colors.

1. Entry hall
2. Dining room
3. Bathroom
4. Bedroom
5. Office
6. Living room
7. Guest bedroom
8. Kitchen

Floor plan

Each piece of furniture has been designed for a specific place in the house and is an intrinsic part of the overall design of the apartment.

D.U.M.B.O. Loft

The original layout of this apartment did not take full advantage of the potential of the space. Natural light is limited, with only two small windows at one end and another at the opposite end of the apartment. The renovation consisted in the removal of the kitchen enclosure to obtain a bright, open space.

Architect: Jeff Etelamaki Design Studio
Location: New York, NY, USA
Year of construction: 2008
Photography: Jeff Etelamaki Design Studio

Floor plan

1. Entry hallway
2. Dining room
3. Living room
4. Office
5. Kitchen
6. Bathroom
7. Bedroom

026

Consider lowering the ceiling height to minimize the width and height disproportion. The dropped ceiling will allow for recessed lighting.

Losa Loft

The remodel of this loft was carried out in two steps: First, the existing space was turned into a neutral white container; second, five architectural elements were strategically inserted—the cradle, the zipper, the hearth, the stage, and the scrim. Each responds to a specific programmatic need.

Architect: Aidlin Darling Design
Location: San Francisco, CA, USA
Year of construction: 2007
Photography: Matthew Millman

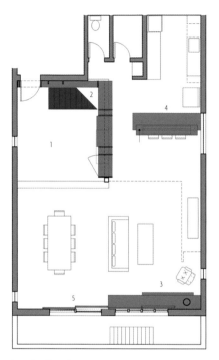

Lower level floor plan

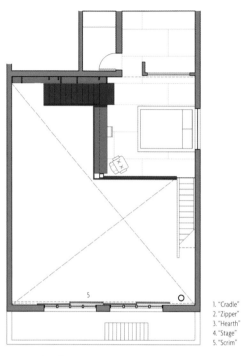

Mezzanine floor plan

1. "Cradle"
2. "Zipper"
3. "Hearth"
4. "Stage"
5. "Scrim"

027

Off-the-shelf items, readily available at any big-box hardware store, are used to build these neatly designed architectural elements.

Cubby House

This project provides additional floor area for a two-story apartment, with a bedroom/study space and new bathroom on the upper level that leaves the lower level to act as the main living space. The living area is designed as a continuous space and features an elevated kitchen floor.

Architect: Edwards Moore
Location: Melbourne, Australia
Year of construction: 2010
Photography: Peter Bennetts

Reclaimed timber, oriented strand board (OSB), sisal, Victorian ash, and white concrete floor create a contrast between sharp lines and rough surfaces.

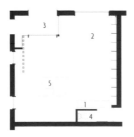

Lower floor plan

Upper floor plan

1. Sliding reflective box
2. Living space
3. Balcony/courtyard
4. Toilet
5. Kitchen
6. Void
7. Pivoting wardrobe
8. Bedroom
9. Bathroom
10. Bath
11. Courtyard

New steelwork provides for a roof
shape with a double-height void running
through the house under a skylight.

028

Oriented strand board (OSB) achieves a strong visual effect at low cost. The surface can be finished with a clear coat, painted matte or gloss.

miniLoft

The goal of this project was to renovate a diminutive Chelsea apartment into a diaphanous, light-filled loft. The focal point of the project is a staircase suspended from the beamed ceiling by a series of delicate cables that accentuate the gracious height of the space while leaving the floor below unimpeded.

Architect: Leone Design Studio
Location: New York, NY, USA
Year of construction: 2006
Photography: Steve Williams

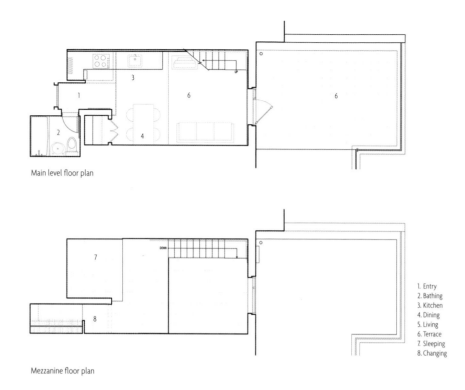

Main level floor plan

Mezzanine floor plan

1. Entry
2. Bathing
3. Kitchen
4. Dining
5. Living
6. Terrace
7. Sleeping
8. Changing

The thick butcher block treads of the
stair play against the fine machine quality
of the stainless steel cable hardware and
railing details.

Home 01

One of the characteristics of this apartment in the center of Amsterdam is its wood "core," which constitutes a centerpiece for the living area. It incorporates the fireplace, TV, and shelves. It also separates the stairs from the living space, creating an intimate atmosphere.

Architect: i29 interior architects
Location: Amsterdam,
the Netherlands
Year of construction: 2007
Photography: i29 interior
architects

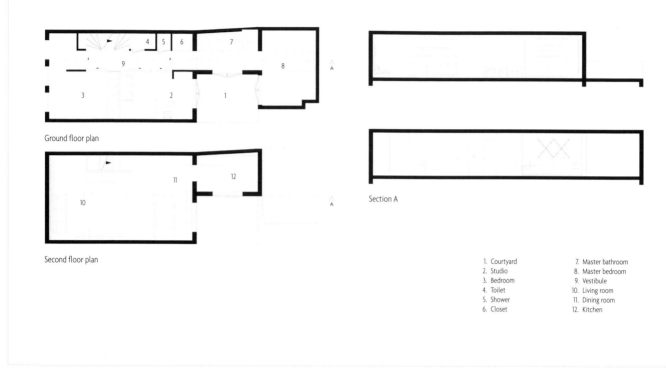

Ground floor plan

Second floor plan

Section A

1. Courtyard
2. Studio
3. Bedroom
4. Toilet
5. Shower
6. Closet

7. Master bathroom
8. Master bedroom
9. Vestibule
10. Living room
11. Dining room
12. Kitchen

The wood core echoes the wood-clad vestibule a floor below. The sliding doors that lead to the various rooms make the vestibule look seamless.

029

Installing the toilet, the sink, and the tub or shower along one wall will facilitate the plumbing and offer opportunities for storage.

Loft Conversion Klostergasse

Architect: Lakonis Architekten
Location: Vienna, Austria
Year of construction: 2008
Photography: Florian Rist,
Margherita Spiluttini, Hertha
Hurnaus

This project consisted of restoring an existing attic and adding a new floor on top of an early 1900's residential building in Vienna. The design concept is built around the idea of a succession of spaces organized on various levels. White and gray tones dominate, enhancing the dynamic architecture.

Upper level floor plan

Lower level floor plan

1. Apartment
2. Elevator
3. Master bedroom
4. Childrens' bedroom
5. Housekeeping
6. Kitchen
7. Living room
8. Dining room
9. Terrace
10. Spa
11. Elevator
12. Herb garden
13. Gallery
14. Open gallery space
15. Upper roof terrace
16. Lower roof terrace

The kitchen, which is directly connected to the herb garden on the upper level by a sheet-metal stair, benefits from abundant natural light.

030

Think of the roof terrace as an outdoor living room. Four key elements to take into account: flooring, plants, furniture, and lighting.

Architect: i29 interior architects
Location: Duivendrecht, the
Netherlands
Year of construction: 2008
Photography: i29 interior
architects

The design concept of this house is centered on providing long sight lines and generous spaces. The living floor has an open structure with openings that lead to other rooms. The sleeping quarters, on the lower floor, present a more intimate plan where the various rooms branch off one side of the hallway.

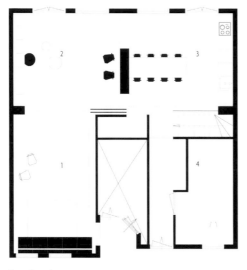

Upper floor plan

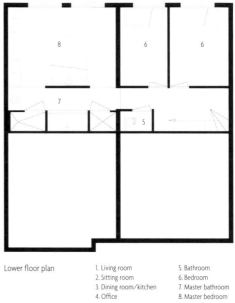

Lower floor plan

1. Living room
2. Sitting room
3. Dining room/kitchen
4. Office
5. Bathroom
6. Bedroom
7. Master bathroom
8. Master bedroom

Two large doors slide across the entire width of the floor plan, which can be divided into smaller, intimate rooms.

031

Before installing wood floorboards, decide which direction the flooring should run to emphasize the length or the width of the room.

032

Wall stickers and decals are a clever solution to animate kids' rooms. They are easy to apply and do not damage the walls.

033

Light colors visually enlarge a room, while dark colors accentuate recessed areas, reinforce depth, and highlight details.

Warm and Classic

Bel-Air

Architect: PTang Studio
Location: Hong Kong, China
Year of construction: 2010
Photography: Ulso Tsang

The designer uses a rich palette of textures and colors, playing with reflections to stimulate the visual experience. This opulence is combined with clever design solutions to fulfill the project's requirements, which called for abundant storage, occasionally hidden behind wall panels, as well as effective lighting.

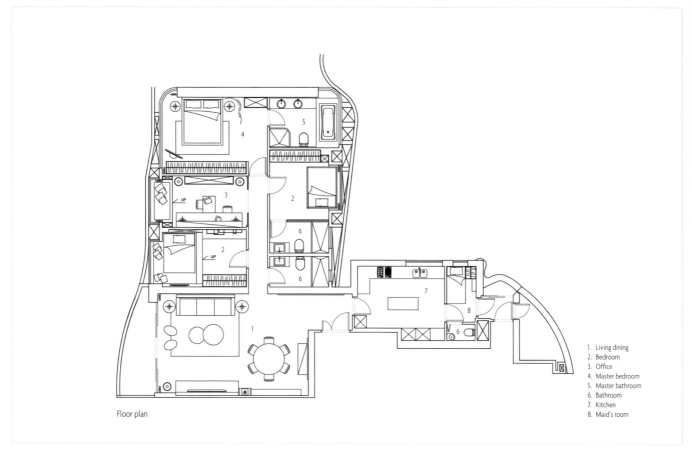

Floor plan

1. Living dining
2. Bedroom
3. Office
4. Master bedroom
5. Master bathroom
6. Bathroom
7. Kitchen
8. Maid's room

A striking wallboard made of thin,
horizontal copper bands designed to
display framed photographs of any size
faces the entry door.

The surfaces in the living and dining area are covered with different textures and colors to achieve a luscious and comfortable atmosphere.

034

Transform unimpressive shelves into stunning displays, grouping objects by theme, color, and shape. Use good lighting as a finishing touch.

035

Spotlights can be the only lighting in a bedroom to highlight certain parts of a wall. If there is a desk, it should have its own work light.

Imperial Penthouse
Mumbai

Architect: Craig Nealy
International
Location: Mumbai, India
Year of construction: 2010
Photography: Craig Nealy
International

This duplex, which occupies half of a floor plate in a tower, is a celebration of the heritage of Indian patterns and craftsmanship. The beauty and variation of this Indian artistic tradition is the decorating theme. The design team also designed every piece of furniture and curated a photography collection.

Ample rooms lavishly finished in pale
gray granite, Carrara marble, and
Venetian plaster are the background
for richly upholstered seating.

Various types of wood were used in the fabrication of the furniture. The simplicity of the design emphasizes the beauty of the natural material.

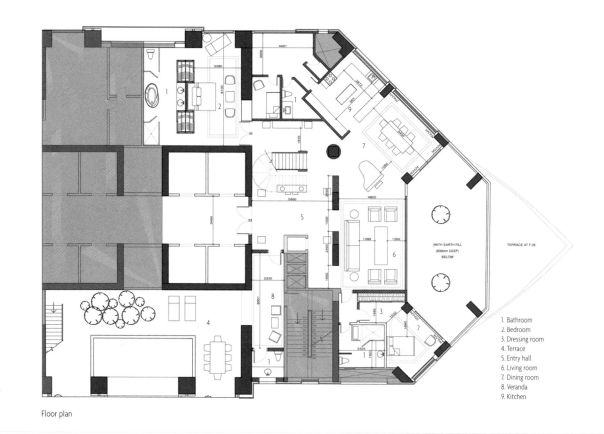

Floor plan

1. Bathroom
2. Bedroom
3. Dressing room
4. Terrace
5. Entry hall
6. Living room
7. Dining room
8. Veranda
9. Kitchen

The bronze stair has Carrara marble treads and leads to a family area on the upper level overlooking the living room below.

036

When decorating a media room, the focus should be on comfort, with smart-home automation controls, appropriate lighting, materials, and finishes.

037

Regardless of the decorating theme for an indoor pool area, be sure to use durable outdoor fabrics.

bedroom 03

library

Palazzo del Mare Residence

This project is one-of-a-kind, as far as the level of freedom that the architects had in designing this home for a trusting client. With few requirements—the color red was a must—the designers splurged on high-quality materials and equipment and experimented with unique architectural features.

Architect: Pepe Calderin Design
Location: Fisher Island, FL, USA
Year of construction: 2009
Photography: Barry Grossman

038

The different parts of the
fireplace, such as the mantel,
the hearth, and the firebox, offer
great opportunities to make a
stunning focal point.

039

Stone veneer is a dimensional wall treatment. Evaluate its decorating potential based on its compatibility with other materials in the room.

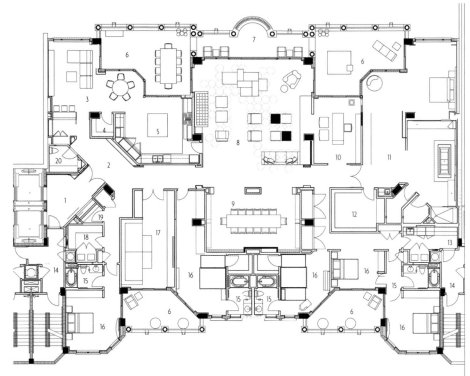

Floor plan

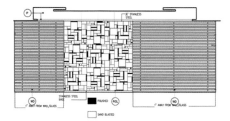

Elevations of the dining room

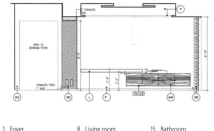

1. Foyer
2. Entry hall
3. Family room
4. Pantry
5. Kitchen
6. Terrace
7. Veranda

8. Living room
9. Dining room
10. Office
11. Master bedroom
12. Dressing room
13. Laundry
14. Service corridor

15. Bathroom
16. Bedroom
17. TV room
18. Trunk room
19. Coat closet
20. Powder room

040

Certain rooms of the house, such as the kitchen and the office, need a flexible combination of ambient, accent, and task lighting.

The use of glass, natural stone, dark woods, and marbles, served as a backdrop for new technologies, like the infinity tub in the master bathroom.

Transparent Loft

Starting with the empty shell of a speculative apartment, the goal was to take advantage of its ample proportions and give it the openness of a loft. The kitchen and master bathroom are enclosed with glass walls, echoing the expanses of glazing on two of the exterior facades and around the recessed terrace.

Architect: Olson Kundig Architects
Location: Seattle, WA, USA
Year of construction: 2007
Photography: Benjamin Benschneider

041

A neutral decor in materials and colors provides a suitable backdrop for the display of art pieces, either hanging on the walls or freestanding.

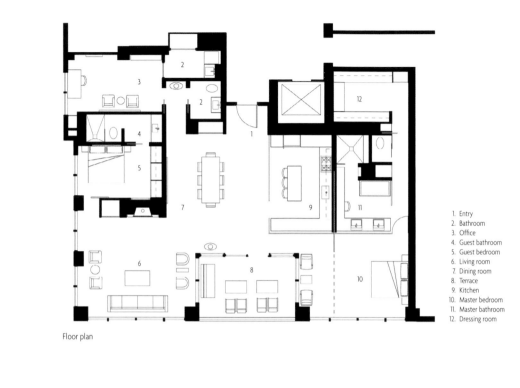

Floor plan

1. Entry
2. Bathroom
3. Office
4. Guest bathroom
5. Guest bedroom
6. Living room
7. Dining room
8. Terrace
9. Kitchen
10. Master bedroom
11. Master bathroom
12. Dressing room

The separation between public and private areas is provided by means of a wall and a sliding screen.

A polished black floor sets off the glass and white walls. The space is warmed by paneling, casework, and the soft upholstered seating.

In the bathroom and in the kitchen, sleek cabinets, mirrors, and metal fittings mounted on the glass appear suspended in the air.

South Beach Retreat

The blue of the ocean was the inspiration throughout this South Beach retreat, while everything else was selected for minimal deviation from this focus. Wide porcelain floors throughout, white walls, and neutral furniture were carefully selected so as not to compete for attention with the views.

Architect: FORMA Design
Location: Miami Beach, FL, USA
Year of construction: 2009
Photography: Geoffrey Hodgdon

Floor plan

1. Entry
2. Dining room
3. Living room
4. Bedroom
5. Master bedroom
6. Master bathroom
7. Bathroom
8. Kitchen
9. Balcony

042

The size and orientation of windows, the transmittance of the glazing, and the reflectance of surfaces affect the quality of day lighting.

At sundown, the blue LED light behind the carved relief wall panels in the living room transforms the space into a Zen lounge.

043

Pebble tiles are available in different sizes and textures. They provide a safe floor to walk on, especially as a base floor for a shower.

044

Different types of fixtures can be used in the same track: from simple incandescent bulbs to halogen designer bulbs and LEDs.

The basic concept of the project consisted of the design of a new, separate apartment as an addition to a 1990s single-story house to accommodate a family with two children. The architects experimented with materials and space to create the formal, yet accommodating, design.

Architect: Lkmk architects
Location: Athens, Greece
Year of construction: 2009
Photography: Louisa Nikolaidou

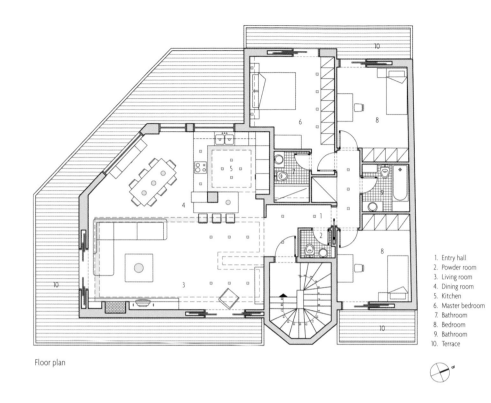

Floor plan

1. Entry hall
2. Powder room
3. Living room
4. Dining room
5. Kitchen
6. Master bedroom
7. Bathroom
8. Bedroom
9. Bathroom
10. Terrace

Luminosity and versatility are the prime objectives of this project, where homogeneity is interrupted by few design features.

The kitchen, dining room, and living area constitute a single space that confers a sense of natural flow.

Natural light pours unobstructed into
the house, becoming the basic unifying
element of the project.

045

Streaks of light accentuate specific objects, while dimmable LED lighting makes for a versatile environment.

Model House

Architect: CJ Studio
Location: Taipei, Taiwan
Year of construction: 2008
Photography: Marc Gerritsen

The design of this apartment introduces a circulation path that links the whole space together while maintaining integral functions for each space. The undulating forms of some of the walls and the furniture make the space welcoming and functionally efficient.

Curvilinear forms soften the space both
in plan and in elevation and harmonize
with the sinuous and circular lines of the
furnishings.

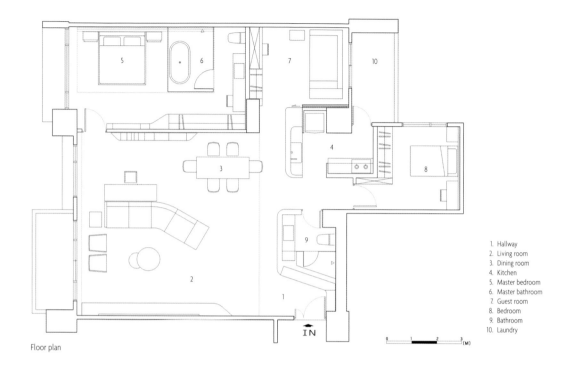

Floor plan

1. Hallway
2. Living room
3. Dining room
4. Kitchen
5. Master bedroom
6. Master bathroom
7. Guest room
8. Bedroom
9. Bathroom
10. Laundry

IN

046

Create areas of demarcation between different activities by using a variety of flooring materials or simply by positioning the same materials in different ways.

047

Take advantage of the extra width in a short hallway or narrow entry to a room to install shelves that will also enliven this underutilized space.

The raised platform, where the bed lays, extends under the glass shower and tub enclosure to facilitate plumbing installation.

X Loft

Architect: Carola Vannini
Architecture
Location: Rome, Italy
Year of construction: 2007
Photography: Filipo Vinardi

Before this old apartment was renovated, its layout consisted of a series of rooms strung along a gloomy corridor. The renovation transformed the apartment into a bright, roomy, and comfortable dwelling that offers interesting perspectives through a striking structure of beams and columns.

048

Color plays an important role in the decoration of a home. Use one color to connect adjacent rooms and give them a strong character.

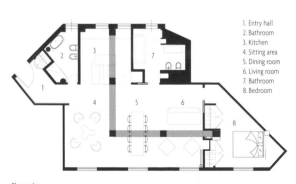

1. Entry hall
2. Bathroom
3. Kitchen
4. Sitting area
5. Dining room
6. Living room
7. Bathroom
8. Bedroom

Floor plan

Model 1

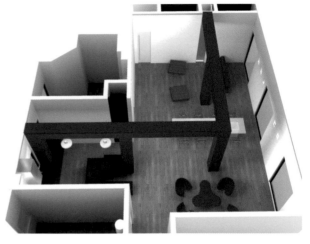

Model 2

Apartment model views

The loft is designed as a place with
seemlessly flowing spaces, guided by the
red structure of beams and columns.

Separated from the living area, the
master bedroom and the bathrooms have
been adapted to the irregular shape of
the apartment.

Casa Micheli

Architect: Simone Micheli
Architectural Hero
Location: Florence, Italy
Year of construction: 2010
Photography: Juergen Eheim

This dynamic intervention transmits originality and vitality within the massive brick walls of a nineteen-century-old building. A brick arch, a remnant of the existing architecture, divides the double-height space into two bays and contrasts with a new inserted volume in the shape of a wedge.

Floor plan

1. Entry
2. Living room
3. Dining room
4. Kitchen
5. Washer and dryer
6. Bedroom
7. Bathroom
8. Master bedroom

The wedge incorporates the kitchen,
a bathroom, and a children's playroom
on the mezzanine and helps direct the
circulation from the entrance.

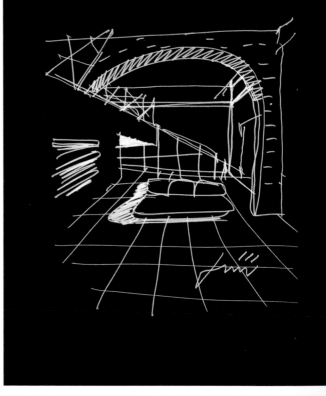

A web made of cord provides security for the children's playroom on the mezzanine while creating an original frieze above the wedge.

The immaculate white space is altered by
a burst of vibrant colors. The acid green
bookshelves, pink sofas, and stair wall
animate the room.

049

Decorating children's bedrooms using a theme and their favorite colors is a great way for them to be able to call it their own.

050

The bedroom should be a comfortable place where all the worries of the day melt away. Appropriate lighting can help set the desired mood.

Apartment in Juhu 2

Architect: KNS Architects and
Sonali Shah
Location: Mumbai, India
Year of construction: 2009
Photography: Rahul Pawar

The design concept of this apartment was to enhance the fluid communication among the different spaces and provide a frame for total unison of mind, body, and soul. The entire design process is based on form finding; the main source of interest being the transition from line to curved surface and curved surface to line.

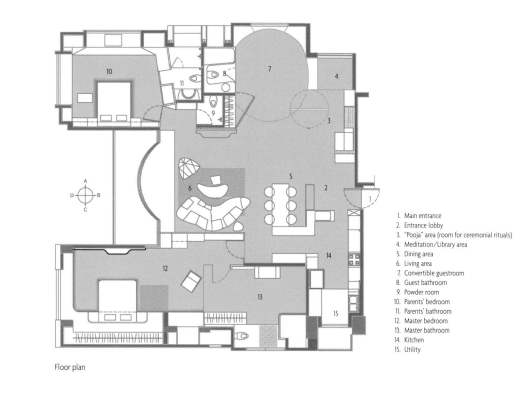

Floor plan

1. Main entrance
2. Entrance lobby
3. "Pooja" area (room for ceremonial rituals)
4. Meditation/Library area
5. Dining area
6. Living area
7. Convertible guestroom
8. Guest bathroom
9. Powder room
10. Parents' bedroom
11. Parents' bathroom
12. Master bedroom
13. Master bathroom
14. Kitchen
15. Utility

The living area is an open space of
generous proportions with a section
that can be closed off and turned into a
guestroom when needed.

Lighting is an intrinsic element of the design, giving the spaces a theatrical atmosphere.

Communication between different functions of the apartment serves as a design opportunity to explore different levels of transparency.

051

Create focal points to avoid monotony. This can be done by drawing attention to a uniquely shaped art piece or with lighting techniques.

052

Incorporate abstract designs with bold paint colors, such as yellow, red, orange, and blue, or other materials to enliven a monochromatic room.

054

When developing your color
scheme, consider patterns and
textures—visual and tactile—of
the fabrics and finishes used in
the design.

055

Design your bathroom around
an art piece that you particularly
like, or turn the room itself into
an artwork. Paint can transform
a bathroom inexpensively.

This house utilizes strong line work and angular planes reinforced by varying lighting effects. The apartment was designed to accommodate the needs of a family of ten. A comfortable 4 BHK apartment had to be converted into 5 BHK along with an entertainment/guest bedroom.

Architect: KNS Architects
Location: Mumbai, India
Year of construction: 2009
Photography: Rahul Pawar

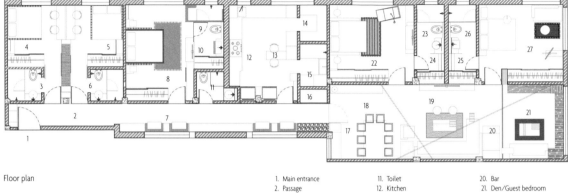

Floor plan

1. Main entrance
2. Passage
3. Children's toilet 1
4. Children's bedroom 1
5. Children's bedroom 2
6. Children's toilet 2
7. Seating
8. Master bedroom 1
9. Master toilet 1
10. Master bedroom 2

11. Toilet
12. Kitchen
13. Breakfast table
14. Storage
15. Utilities
16. Storage
17. "Mandir" (Hindu or Jain temple)
18. Dining area
19. Living area

20. Bar
21. Den/Guest bedroom
22. Master bedroom 2
23. Master toilet 2
24. Walk-in closet
25. Walk-in closet
26. Master toilet 3
27. Master bedroom 3

056

Add unique touches to a bathroom by painting one wall to go with the design theme in the rest of the house.

Private Residence

This spacious apartment features light-colored finishes on all the surfaces, emphasizing a blend of textures and shades that work in counterpoint to the home's sleek furniture selection. Inspired by the yin and yang, the design achieves an elegant and understated effect that evokes a relaxed atmosphere.

Architect: CL3 Architects
Location: Shanghai, China
Year of construction: 2009
Photography: Nirut Benjabanpot

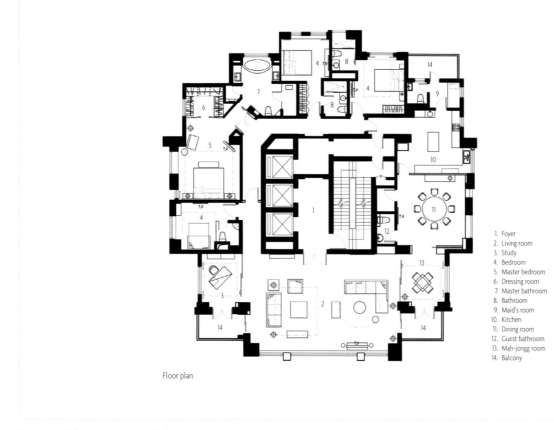

Floor plan

1. Foyer
2. Living room
3. Study
4. Bedroom
5. Master bedroom
6. Dressing room
7. Master bathroom
8. Bathroom
9. Maid's room
10. Kitchen
11. Dining room
12. Guest bathroom
13. Mah-jongg room
14. Balcony

The layout of the apartment, organized around the staircase and elevator core, allows for every room to have a window or access to a balcony.

057

Monotones are varying tones of one color, and in most cases constitute safe schemes to paint a room. Be careful not to fall into monotony!

058

The inclusion of a dressing room in the en suite room will free up armoire and dresser space in the bedroom.

Residence Tsai's

The dining room, sitting area, and master bedroom in this apartment are aligned and connected by means of a continuous vaulted ceiling. Glossy and matte finishes of the same white shade combine with mirrored surfaces to emphasize the sense of amplitude and continuity between the different spaces.

Architect: CJ Studio
Location: Taipei, Taiwan
Year of construction: 2009
Photography: Marc Gerritsen

059

When entertaining, a kitchen-area island allows the cook to keep in visual and conversational contact with the adjoining eating place.

060

Screens provide visual separation between different areas and can fulfill other functions, such as providing a hanging surface for artwork.

061

When planning an en suite master bedroom, decide on the location of the bedroom, the bathroom, and the walk-in closet relative to each other.

062

Create low partitions throughout the room to break up large open spaces, and use translucent materials so the room remains somewhat open.

The remodel of this attic takes reference from the concept of a dormer window. On a formal level, the triangulation of the roof plane gives shape to the ceilings, walls, and new staircase. On a programmatic level, it allows for other functional needs of the apartment, such as lighting and ventilation.

Wulumuqi Road Apartment

Architect: SKEW Collaborative
Location: Shanghai, China
Year of construction: 2009
Photography:
Shen Photo

063

Special attention should be given to lighting around mirrors in the bathroom to avoid glare, awkward reflections, or insufficient lighting.

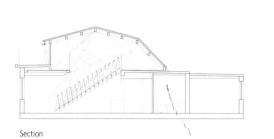

Section

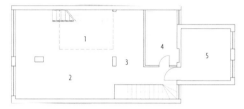

Lower level floor plan

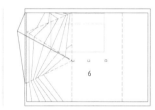

Mezzanine floor plan and reflected ceiling plan

1. Dining room
2. Living room
3. Kitchen
4. Bathroom
5. Bedroom
6. Studio

The rest of the apartment was kept relatively simple to let the folding surfaces and the stair take center stage.

Mixed-use Townhouse

This two-story apartment sits on top of a garage and a single retail tenant at street level. The living spaces are on the second floor, surrounding a courtyard, while the third floor contains bedrooms and a large exterior dining and entertainment deck with views over the ocean.

Architect: Dennis Gibbens Architects
Location: Venice, CA, USA
Year of construction: 2008
Photography: Dennis Gibbens Architects, Nazy Alvarez

The entire shell of the building, which is constructed of board-formed, poured-in-place concrete, is exposed in the interior of the apartment.

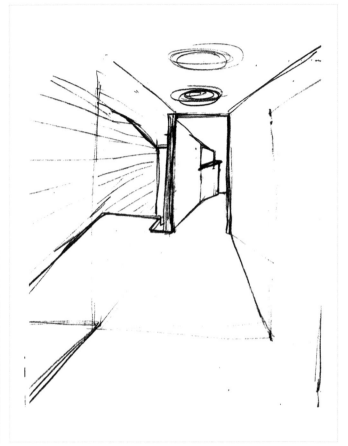

The rough texture of the concrete contrasts with the smooth finish of the stone, stainless steel, stained woods, and terrazzo floors.

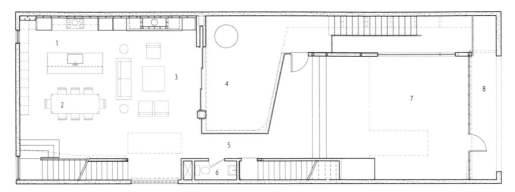

Lower level floor plan

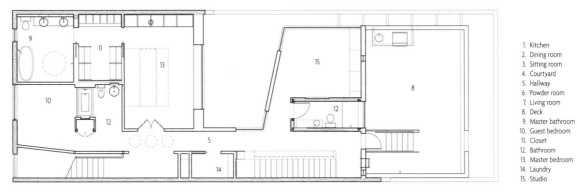

Upper level floor plan

1. Kitchen
2. Dining room
3. Sitting room
4. Courtyard
5. Hallway
6. Powder room
7. Living room
8. Deck
9. Master bathroom
10. Guest bedroom
11. Closet
12. Bathroom
13. Master bedroom
14. Laundry
15. Studio

064

An important advantage of inner courtyards is that they offer an open-air feeling and allow interior spaces to expand outward on good, warm days.

065

To create an unusual bathroom, start with a freestanding tub. Install it against a nice stone wall or on a precious marble plinth.

Porthole Loft

This industrial loft is transformed into a three-bedroom home. Remnants of the existing timber frame and structural brick walls are expressed as part of the architecture. The kitchen, bathrooms, and utility room are organized into a core box that emits light to the adjacent spaces.

Architect: Desai / Chia Architecture
Location: New York, NY, USA
Year of construction: 2008
Photography: Paul Warchol Photography

1. Entry hall
2. Bedroom
3. Bathroom
4. Kitchen
5. Laundry
6. Living/dining

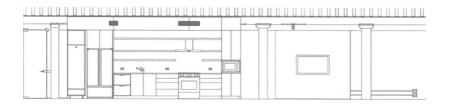

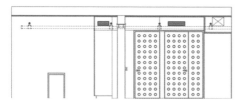
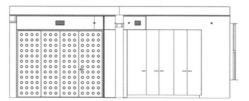

Floor plan and interior elevations

066

In open-plan spaces, sliding panels easily transform a space by allowing areas to be sectioned off for privacy or opened up, as needed.

Porthole Loft **307**

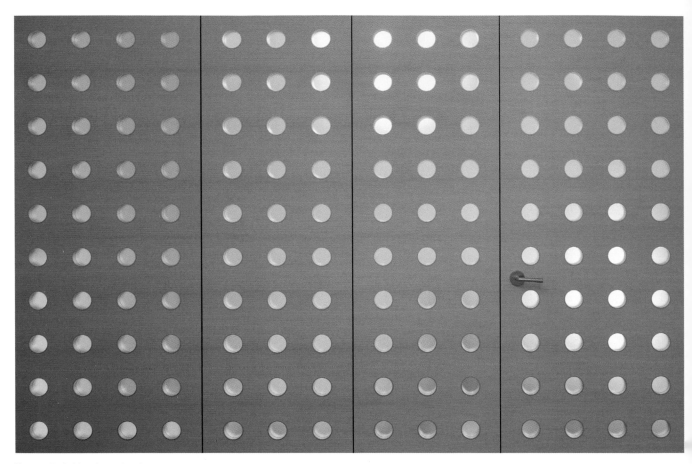

The core is clad in ash wood and
perforated with anodized aluminum
portholes. Translucent acrylic discs are
inserted into each porthole.

The portholes create a dynamic pattern on the surface of the core and allow light through while still maintaining privacy.

Kaneko Loft

The clients and their extensive art collection find a new home in the large space within an old brick and concrete warehouse building located in the Old Market District of downtown Omaha. The sparse aesthetic of refurbished steel, brick, and concrete forms the backdrop for living and entertaining.

Architect: MACK Architect(s)
Location: Omaha, NE, USA
Year of construction: 2009
Photography: Takashi Hatekeyama

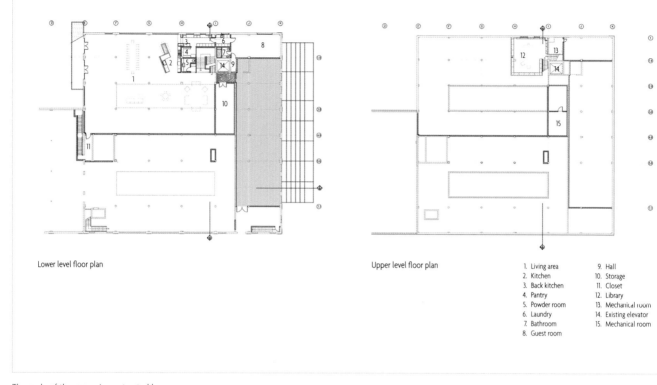

Lower level floor plan

Upper level floor plan

1. Living area
2. Kitchen
3. Back kitchen
4. Pantry
5. Powder room
6. Laundry
7. Bathroom
8. Guest room
9. Hall
10. Storage
11. Closet
12. Library
13. Mechanical room
14. Existing elevator
15. Mechanical room

The scale of the space is contrasted by
the precise articulation of programmatic
areas for cooking, dining, reading,
bathing, and sleeping.

The architectural interventions within the space are kept minimal in order to allow the extraordinary large-scale space to take center stage.

Bespoke casework wraps around existing columns, and new "boxes" are inserted in the bare industrial shell to emphasize its original use as a warehouse.

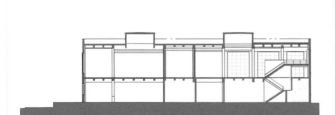

Section

J-Loft

Architect: Plystudio
Location: Singapore, Singapore
Year of construction: 2008
Photography: Stzernstudio

This typical post-war attic was remodeled to meet the client's particular needs. The interior walls were removed to create an open plan. The architects came up with different design strategies to define the different spaces. In the end, they opted for a series of wood boxes in a linear arrangement.

The structures take up 6.5 ft of the apartment's 20 ft width. The only enclosing structures are the doors used to close off the private areas.

067

Knocking down the walls that separate the different rooms enables more daylight to illuminate the interior and facilitates fluid circulation.

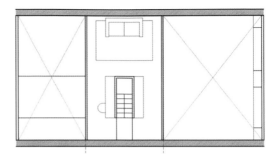

Mezzanine floor plan

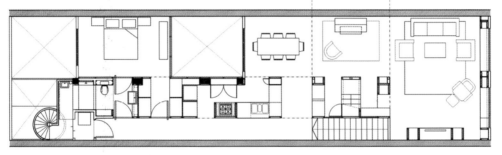

Ground floor plan

The structures, entirely fabricated in plywood, allow for a visual connection between the different areas and offer interesting perspectives.

Graph

The occupant of this apartment works as a camerawoman in the film and television world. A long corridor leads to the different rooms of the house, which includes a workspace in addition to the common living areas. The originality of this apartment is in its furnishings and dramatic lighting.

Architect: Apollo Architects & Associates
Location: Tokyo, Japan
Year of construction: 2006
Photography: Masao Nishikawa

Graph 327

The linear space of the hall successfully accommodates the workbench. The darkroom is conveniently located near the kitchen and the workbench.

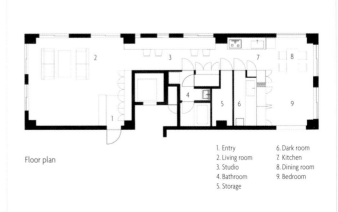

Floor plan

1. Entry
2. Living room
3. Studio
4. Bathroom
5. Storage
6. Dark room
7. Kitchen
8. Dining room
9. Bedroom

068

Good lighting above the work area is critical. Fluorescents or LEDs are good options.

Graph **329**

Aluminum House

This apartment is located in a former office building. Few changes were made to the original layout: A layer of different depths along the perimeter of the space accommodated the entire program, which includes a workbench, a kitchenette, closets, shelves, and a bathroom around the large, open room.

Architect: Hideki Yoshimatsu &
Archipro Architects
Location: Yokohama, Japan
Year of construction: 2008
Photography: Archipro
Architects

The distinctive texture of the pine wood flooring was achieved by hammering its surface uniformly.

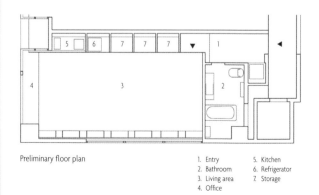

Preliminary floor plan

1. Entry
2. Bathroom
3. Living area
4. Office
5. Kitchen
6. Refrigerator
7. Storage

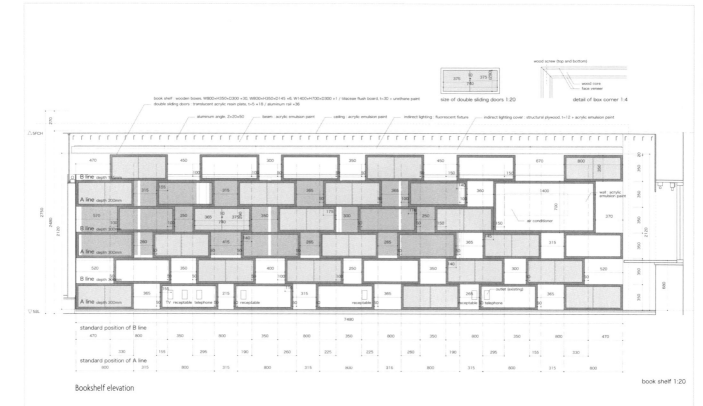

wood screw (top and bottom)

375 / 10 / 375 / 780

wood core
face veneer

size of double sliding doors 1:20

detail of box corner 1:4

book shelf : wooden boxes, W800×H350×D300 ×30, W800×H350×D145 ×6, W1400×H700×D300 ×1 / tiliaceae flush board, t=30 + urethane paint
double sliding doors : translucent acrylic resin plate, t=5 ×18 / aluminum rail ×36

aluminum angle, 2×20×50 — beam : acrylic emulsion paint — ceiling : acrylic emulsion paint — indirect lighting : fluorescent fixture — indirect lighting cover : structural plywood, t=12 + acrylic emulsion paint

△5FCH
270

470 / 450 / 300 / 350 / 450 / 670 / 800

20
350
350

B line depth 145mm
100 / 100 / 50 / 50 / 150 / 150

315 / 155 / 315 / 365 / 365 / 140 / 360 / 1400

wall : acrylic emulsion paint

A line depth 200mm
50 / 50 / 100 / 100

350

air conditioner

570 / 100 / 365 / 10 / 375 / 350 / 175 / 300 / 250 / 150 / 150

370

2750
2480
2120

B line depth 300mm
100 / 50 / 50 / 50 / 50 / 150

260 / 415 / 140 / 265 / 265 / 365 / 145 / 315

A line depth 300mm
50 / 50 / 50 / 50 / 150

520 / 350 / 400 / 250 / 350 / 140 / 300 / 520

B line depth 300mm
50 / 100 / 100 / 50

365 / 155 / 215 / 315 / 365 / 265 / 365

outlet (existing)

A line depth 300mm
50 / TV receptacle / telephone 50 / 50 receptable / 50 / receptacle 50 / receptacle 50 telephone

2120
350 / 350 / 350 / 350 / 680

▽5SL

7490

standard position of B line
470 / 800 / 350 / 800 / 350 / 800 / 350 / 800 / 350 / 800 / 350 / 800 / 470

330 / 155 / 295 / 190 / 260 / 225 / 225 / 260 / 190 / 295 / 155 / 330

standard position of A line
800 / 315 / 800 / 315 / 800 / 315 / 800 / 315 / 800 / 315 / 800 / 315 / 800

Bookshelf elevation

book shelf 1:20

069

A series of boxes of different sizes can be stacked to create a shelving unit to make the most of a disused wall in the house.

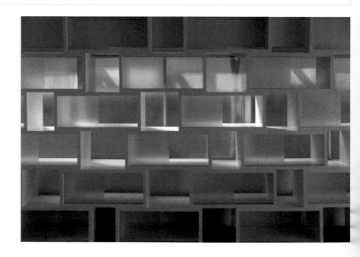

070

Black can be more than just an accent color. Bathrooms take black well. Combined with white, black creates a dramatic and elegant effect.

Living Pod

Located in the center of Hong Kong, this apartment, with a multilayered and intrinsic design, presents a contemporary living pattern as an alternative to the traditional home. It aims to represent how the city life influences our living space, and in return, how the space shapes our way of living.

Architect: Joey Ho Design
Location: Hong Kong, China
Year of construction: 2008
Photography: Graham Uden, Ray Lau

Floor plan

1. Entry
2. Living
3. Dining
4. Bar
5. Maid's room
6. Kitchen
7. Bathroom
8. Bedroom
9. Study
10. Master bedroom
11. Master bathroom

The strong graphic theme applied to every room enhances a sense of depth that animates the otherwise flat surfaces of the apartment.

071

Rope lights are often mounted under cabinets and also behind any opaque surface, providing subtle visual effects in any room of the house.

Layers of transparent glass and mirrors help connect all the rooms while projecting and reflecting the imagery of the marine theme.

The rooms in the apartment are visible through layers of glass doors and interior windows. To further accentuate the effect of lightness and spaciousness, the color palette is limited to white with accents of bright colors. Views of the natural surroundings inspired the apartment's decorating theme.

Architect: **PTang Studio**
Location: **Hong Kong, China**
Year of construction: **2010**
Photography: **Ulso Tsang**

A floral pattern on the door closet is carved into the wood, giving the impression that the surface has been pushed in.

Chet Bakerstraat

This apartment has undergone an extensive remodel. Partitions are kept to a minimum. A tall and long cabinet delimits the different areas and organizes the circulation. Light colors and natural materials predominate, unifying the spaces and enhancing the sense of spaciousness and functionality.

Architect: Hofman Dujardin Architects
Location: Amsterdam, the Netherlands
Year of construction: 2008
Photography: Matthijs van Roon

Floor plan

1. Foyer
2. Terrace
3. Living room
4. Dining room
5. Kitchen
6. Den/Guest bedroom
7. Master bedroom
8. Master bathroom
9. Bathroom

The bathroom and storage area block
off the living space, creating definition
between the rest of the rooms of the
apartment and the terrace.

074

The feeling of spaciousness is achieved by avoiding upper cabinets in the kitchen, which integrates well with the living and dining room.

075

On cabinet and closet doors, use recessed edge pulls in lieu of regular knobs for a clean homogenous look.

Plantage Kerklaan

This apartment is one large, open space where the different areas are separated by partitions with no doors. This creates a sense of spaciousness despite the reduced area. The built-in cabinets and the kitchen island fulfill their functions while at the same time serving to organize the different zones.

Architect: Hofman Dujardin Architects
Location: Amsterdam, the Netherlands
Year of construction: 2008
Photography: Matthijs van Roon

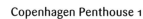

Copenhagen Penthouse 1

The clients, who often travel, wanted an apartment with a simple design that would be ideal for relaxation. All architectural features were simplified to a maximum: Built-in cabinets, sliding doors, and lit niches throughout are designed to minimize the need for unnecessary items, such as lamps and furnishings.

Architect: **Norm.Architects**
Location: **Copenhagen, Denmark**
Year of construction: **2009**
Photography: **Norm.Architects**

Concealed lighting from Agabekov was also mounted in the white and travertine bathroom to enhance its minimalistic design.

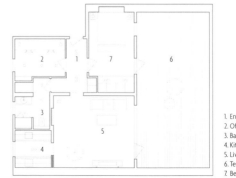

1. Entry
2. Office
3. Bathroom
4. Kitchen
5. Living/dining
6. Terrace
7. Bedroom

Floor plan

Copenhagen Penthouse 2

The interior of this penthouse has been completely redone. The design required several walls to be torn down in order to obtain an open plan. The different spaces are organized around a central core. A flat screen is mounted on one side of the core, while the opposite side provides access to storage.

Architect: **Norm.Architects**
Location: **Copenhagen, Denmark**
Year of construction: **2009**
Photography: **Jonas Bjerre-Poulsen**

A white resin floor was cast to homogenize the space and to emphasize the presence of the central core, which is painted matte black.

A lighting cove was installed at the base of the core. The structure appears to hover above the floor and conveys a sense of lightness.

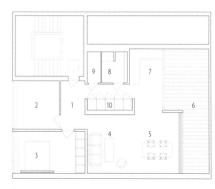

Floor plan

1. Entry
2. Guest bedroom
3. Master bedroom
4. Living room
5. Dining room
6. Terrace
7. Kitchen
8. Bathroom
9. Storage
10. Closet

078

Door openings that extend to the ceiling create an open plan and increase the feeling of height.

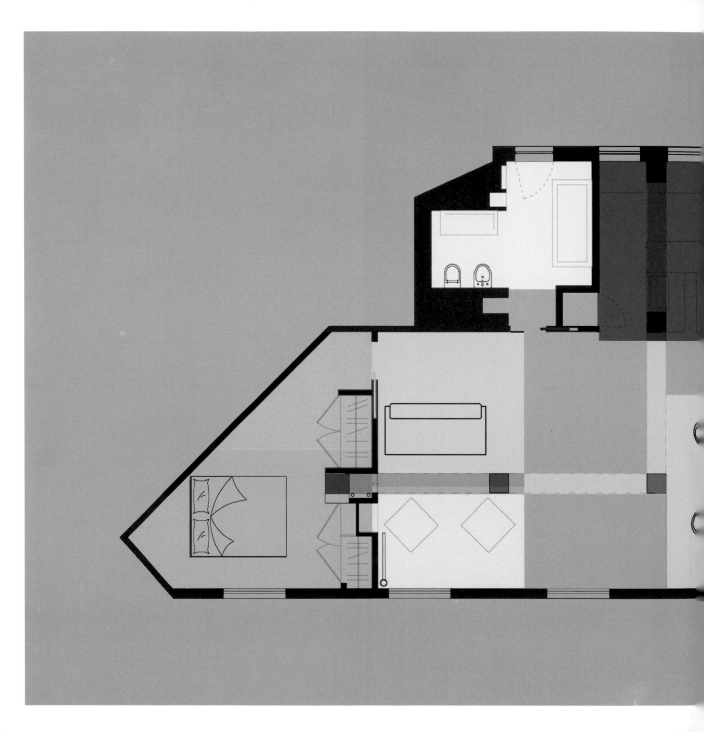

Room by Room

Living

079

To optimize space in pitched-roof attics with limited headroom, consider adequate furniture placement and built-ins.

The contrasting color of the island separates the kitchen from the dining area while creating a harmonic color link with the living room.

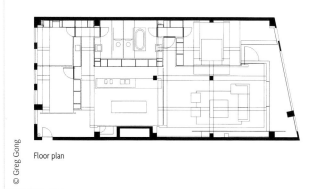

Floor plan

© Greg Gong

Greg Gong / © John Gollings

Greg Gong / John Collings

To break up the linearity of the space, the
pieces of furniture have been arranged
in clusters that correspond to different
functions.

080

Different ceiling heights and floor levels help delimit the various functions, with no need for furniture to act as dividers.

A reveal at the bottom and at the top of a wall creates the illusion of floor and ceiling continuity.

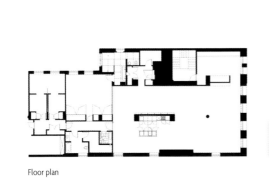

Floor plan

081

Simple roll-up shades are a good solution for light control and privacy. They provide a clean finish to a minimalistic decoration.

The flue of this freestanding fireplace is
concealed behind a row of wall cabinets,
which provides storage and frees up
floor space.

i29 interior architects / © i29 interior architects

The brick walls and the polished concrete floor contrast with the white shell and harmonize with the eclectic selection of furniture.

The flat screen, sound system, and air-conditioning supply registers are integrated into a wall-surface treatment above the fireplace.

The columns help organize the different
functions of this open-plan apartment.
The selection of neutral colors reinforces
the space.

082

When hanging artwork of different sizes and shapes together, consider grouping, spacing, and positioning relative to the wall.

© MOLTENI

083

Select large-scale pieces of
furniture for tall rooms to avoid
an awkward disproportion.

© MOLTENI

Modular bookshelf units allow for a customized composition that fits any storage necessity.

Suspended wood ceiling panels integrate lighting and air conditioning systems while balancing out the wood floor and the cabinets.

The long cabinet under the windowsill permits a clean layout of the room and accentuates the minimalist design of the windows.

084

Smooth high-gloss resin flooring
is ideal for a contemporary look
that is durable and easy to clean.

Floor plan

Agustí Costa / © David Cardelús

Agustí Costa / © David Cardelús

085

The space furthest from the center of a pitched-roof attic is used to install a low cabinet system in a color similar to that of the walls.

086

Cove lighting is used to emphasize the shape and treatment of a wall clad in natural stone while setting pleasant mood lighting for the room.

The design of this room focuses on the rich palette of colors, materials, and textures and minimizes the use of decorative objects.

Pascal Arquitectos / © Sófocles Hernández

A horizontal reveal halfway up the wall creates a focal point below eye level to visually lower the ceiling and make the room cozier.

Floor plan

This simple bookshelf is lightweight, sturdy, and infinitely expandable to create a dynamic pattern that animates your living room.

© LAGO

These storage units come in different colors of opaque glass. The different sizes allow for creative configuration.

087

Playing with geometric shapes, vivid colors, and innovative materials helps to create original solutions without sacrificing practical aspects.

A TV screen that expands and retracts
in front of your TV is the ultimate
technological device for an entertainment
center environment.

This wall unit is formed by modular items that can be organized around your living room's AV equipment.

© MOLTEN

Modular furniture systems combine
shape, material, and color, forming any
configuration that suits your spatial
needs and decorating ideas.

088

A nice bookshelf can easily be used as a room divider. The trick is to not fill in the shelves completely so as to be able to see through them.

This wall unit incorporates a flat screen TV into its design. The front panel with the TV slides along a track in front of a shelf.

© MODÀ

© MODÀ

Sleek and striking, this entertainment
center unit is the ultimate finishing touch
for your ultramodern living room.

Kitchens

While an open kitchen is integrated in the living area, the main kitchen, equipped with all the bulky appliances, is located in another room.

Norm Architects / © Jonas Bjerre-Poulsen

091

A one-wall kitchen can efficiently incorporate all the basic appliances. Storage may be resolved by having a pantry nearby with easy access.

The living area and the kitchen are physically connected but visually separated by means of a change in the flooring material.

Miró Rivera Architects / © Paul Finkel

Miró Rivera Architects / © Paul Finkel

This kitchen remodel utilizes a simple palette of materials that maintain a balance between the original elements and the modern reforms.

The kitchen is visually and physically connected to the exterior, very convenient for having meals in the yard during the summer.

Floor plan

Feldman Architecure / © Paul Dyer

092

Open shelves against a glass
exterior wall or a window
between a countertop and upper
cabinets provide backlighting
and an interesting display.

The double-height ceilings are exploited
to obtain a spacious kitchen. Key features
include two parallel work areas and an
imposing flue.

The kitchen of this small apartment is hidden behind sliding panels along one wall to keep the living area tidy and uncluttered.

093

An expansive walnut and
bamboo kitchen island organizes
the space, allowing for a tidy
and clean living experience.

Some small drawers and electrical outlets are conveniently installed on the island's countertop, away from children's reach.

Rustic materials and exposed industrial
hardware and appliances were utilized to
create a casual, warm atmosphere and to
unify the space.

094

Before you decide to install an island that requires a vent hood, consider the ceiling height and possibly a vent stack installation.

The remodel of an existing gloomy
kitchen resulted in a harmonious space
for family activities.

095

Organize the appliances you use most frequently in easy to access places. Appliance garages help to keep a less cluttered countertop.

© DADA

096

Be creative when it comes to storage: Add additional shelving for utensils, and place spice racks between the countertop and the upper cabinets.

© BULTHAUP

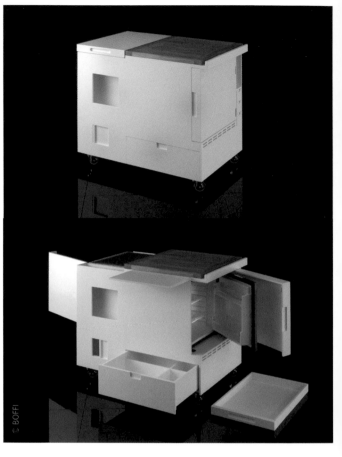

097

If your kitchen is too small to accommodate all its needed functions in a conventional layout, consider a compact kitchen, which can maximize efficiency.

Luxury kitchen designs combine highly
functional hardware and details with
high-quality materials, creating value
over the long term.

In addition to high-quality appliances, cabinetry is an important investment in any new or remodeled kitchen interested in maximizing storage capacity.

© ERNESTO MEDA

© ERNESTO MEDA

Tall pull-out cabinets make the best use of space and make it so it's less necessary have to reach to the back of your cabinets.

© ERNESTO MEDA

Cabinets can be easily retrofitted with narrow pullout shelving units to optimize organization.

Home Offices

101

For rooms with high ceilings or double-height spaces, invest in tall bookshelves and a library ladder to reach books on the highest shelves.

© MOLTENI

102

Take advantage of large floor-to-ceiling windows to benefit from abundant natural light in your office.

Aidlin Darling Design / © John Sutton

Agustí Costa / © David Cardelús

103

In addition to solving issues of lack of storage, a custom-made shelf unit can become an integral part of the apartment design.

Dwellers of small spaces often optimize the utility of the dining table by also using it as a work desk. The best desks are dining tables!

BUILD / © BUILD

The office is separated from the living area by a sliding door, which can be kept open for additional space.

This desk makes a striking effect as the centerpiece in any room of the house. Minimal decoration should only enhance its beauty.

© DO+CE

© RÖ

104

A writing (or computer) desk can come in handy for keeping an unsightly computer out of the way in the living area.

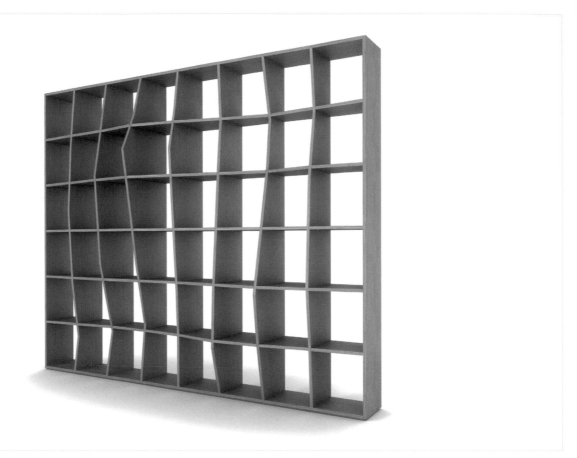

105

Striking designs of bookcases and bookshelf units encourage minimal and spacious room-design concepts.

106

Creative wall-decorating ideas can be utilized as shelving space, combining artistic taste and functionality.

107

This bookcase, fabricated in sheet metal, comes in various finishes and allows infinite possibilities of configuration.

The beauty of this writing desk is in its minimalistic silhouette and sleek, glossy finish—a practical piece of furniture that fits anywhere.

108

Creating a work space in the
entry hall of the apartment is a
good option for making better
use of a typically misused space.

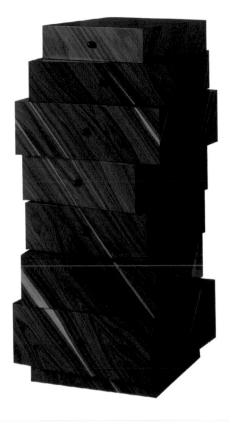

109

Pieces of furniture that conceal a writing desk are ideal for those who don't need one on a daily basis and so don't want to have it exposed.

These designs allow for integrating the working space into a room with multiple uses without interfering with other activities.

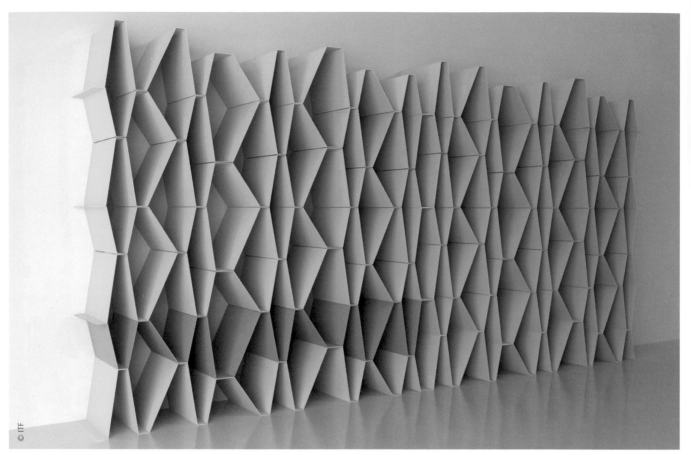

110

These eye-catching and atypical shelving units can be just what you need if you are looking for fun, decorative ideas.

© ZANOTTA

111

Inspired by Piet Mondrian's well-known artwork, these shelf units bring an artistic taste to your home office.

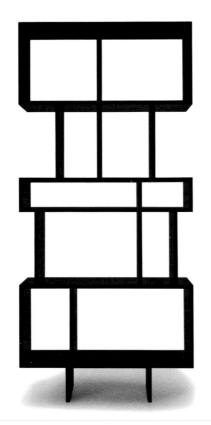

© EMMEMOBILI

112

Creative shelving units of different configurations allow arrangement of CDs and books to accommodate the user's storage needs.

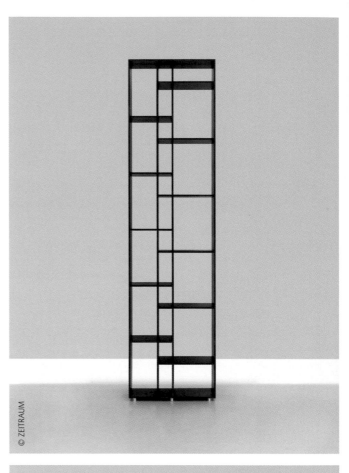

© ZEITRAUM

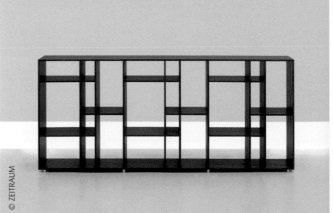

© ZEITRAUM

© EMMEBI

© OFFECCT

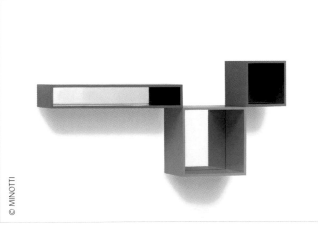

© MINOTTI

113

Choose the colors, furniture, and accessories with care so that your office doesn't become the neglected corner in your home.

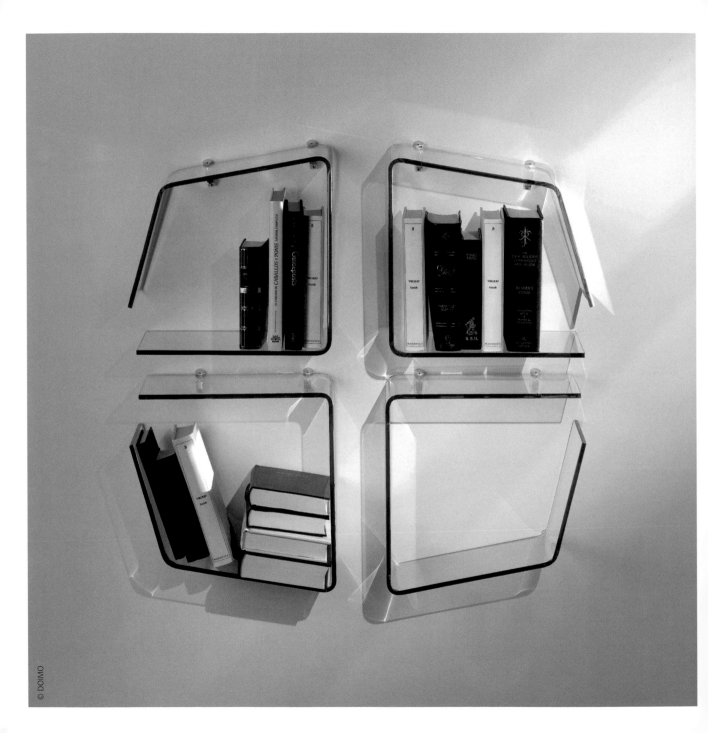

© XAM

© MINOTTI

© SINTESI

114

Decorating the office is as easy as any other room. Come up with a concept and select all the furniture and accessories accordingly.

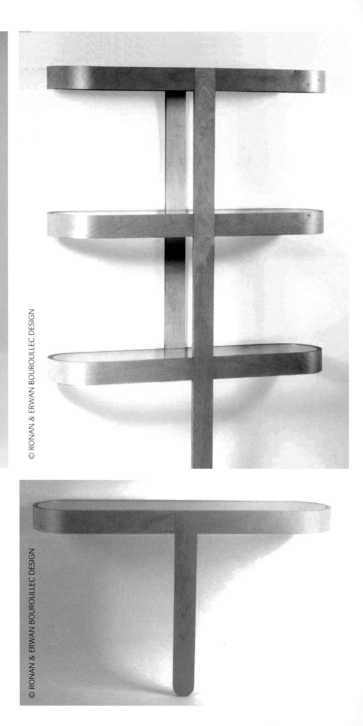

115

No need to shop for everything at once. As with any other room, take it slow in order to progressively achieve the feel that you want.

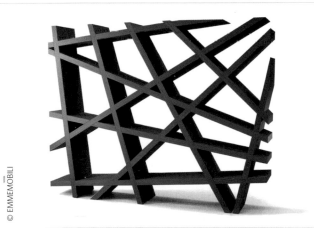

Unique designs are available in any style, form, and finish to help create a pleasant home office environment while avoiding conventionalism.

Bedrooms

A rustic-style console lavatory is located in the bedroom, fitting perfectly with the bed and bench of the same style.

A deep windowsill integrates a long built-in cabinet, fulfilling the need for additional closet space and accentuating the linearity of the room.

© Archive

116

Show off your en suite sitting area and give the master bedroom more space by using an open-plan design.

The bed takes center stage in this sophisticated master bedroom that illustrates sensual comfort reinforced with dramatic lighting.

117

Heavy velvet, mohair, cashmere, silk and satin, or airy, sheer fabrics, cotton, and linen must be pleasant to the eye and soft to the touch.

A play of curves and colors from the dresser to the bathroom mirror contributes to the magic feeling of this bedroom.

FORMA Design / © Geoffrey Hodgson

118

The bed in this bedroom is low so as not to dominate the space. A low bed is a must if the ceiling is particularly low or pitched.

CJ Studio / © Marc Gerritsen

This headboard extends the entire length
of the wall and doubles as a nightstand
and a computer desk.

119

An irregularity in the existing shape of the room can be used to create a *Tokonoma*-inspired niche above the bed with built-in lights.

120

Fold-down bunk beds are convenient space-saving furniture for small apartments and studios and a great solution for guest rooms.

© SMART BEDS

121

The layout of the room varies depending on the use: Use hideaway beds for the occasional visitors, or have a sofa as part of your regular room plan.

A low partition separates the living area from the bedroom, creating an open plan that takes advantage of daylight and views.

122

Indulge yourself by creating a room that is not only functional but also is one that you can call your own private space in the house.

123

Modular furnishings such as shelves, baskets, and rails are good solutions to make the dressing room as functional as possible.

MB Studio-Sistema MIDI / © MB Studio

© DOIMO

124

If room allows, find a large comfortable chair and an ottoman or a chaise longue to relax on while getting ready.

125

The slide-out hanging rails and baskets permit easy access to garments for everyday use while keeping everything organized.

© BELLIGOTTI

126

While some homes lack storage space, others have spare room. Turn this unused space into your very own dressing room.

This combination—headboard on one side and shelf unit on the opposite side—makes an efficient space divider for a studio apartment.

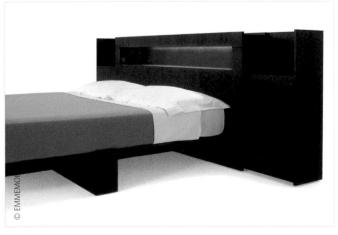

This Murphy bed on wheels can easily be
stored away completely, turned around
to make space to fold down a desk, or
both can be in use.

Convenient for temporarily setting up an office space, this shelf unit closes itself to look like a large, nicely finished trunk.

Innovative designs that incorporate
various functions into one unit make
the most of reduced spaces, allowing
flexibility in the room layout.

This bed spins around from behind a bookshelf. Long gone are the early Murphy beds, with their ugly fronts.

The sofa bed idea has been around for decades, but this simple design uses a clever tie system to bring out what is essential in the concept.

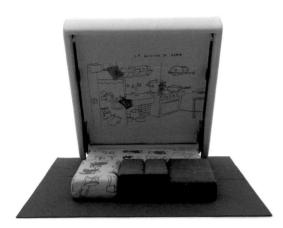

The design of space-saving furniture evolves to further simplify their use while improving functionality and versatility.

Kids' Rooms

Furniture for kids' rooms allows for much greater freedom in design, so long as the pieces are functional, sturdy, versatile, colorful, and safe.

129

Functions such as studying, sleeping, and storing are combined to result in clever solutions that make the most of reduced spaces.

Steps and ladders are devices integrated into the design of furniture with the objective being to make the bedroom a place where kids want to be.

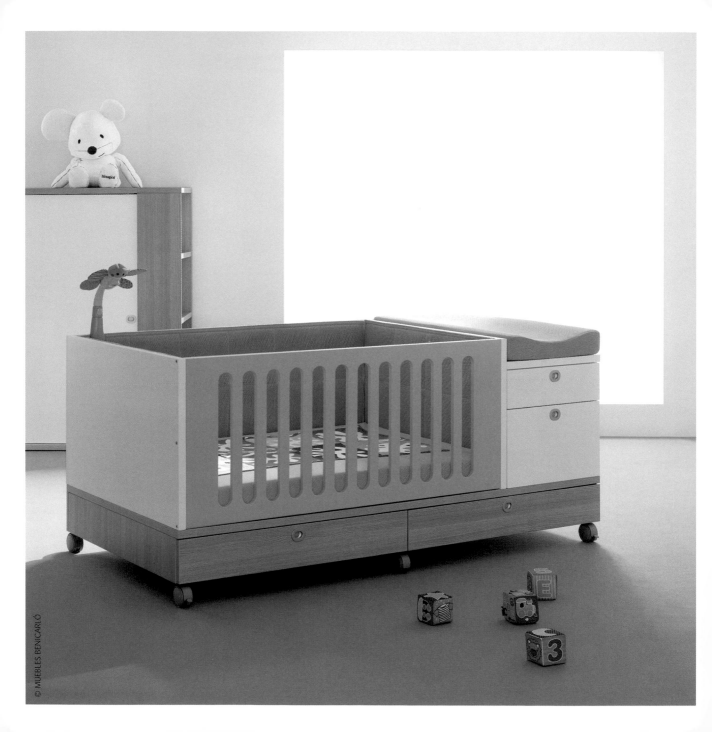

130

Pieces of furniture that integrate various functions not only save space but also facilitate tasks such as changing, storing, and sleeping.

Reds and oranges are in the warm-color group. They are inviting, stimulating, cheerful, and dynamic.

131

Becoming familiar with the effects that different colors have on our minds will help decide what tones are most appropriate for our children.

132

Bring excitement to a bedroom by using contrasting color schemes. Use one color and accent it with its opposite tone in the color wheel.

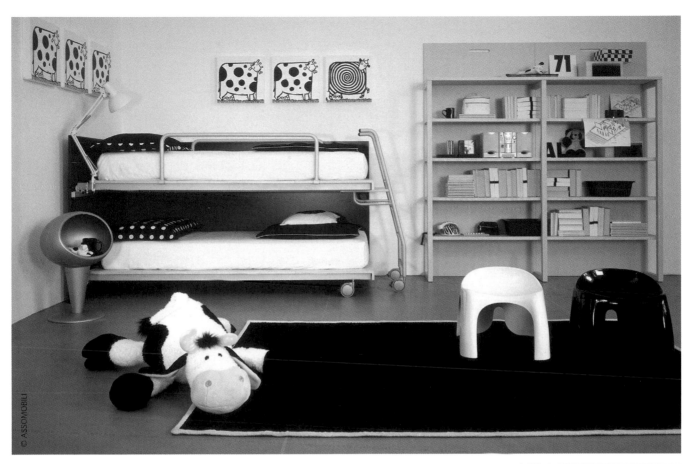

© ASSOMOBILI

Remember that a favorite color might be overwhelming on its own but is very manageable when combined with neutral colors.

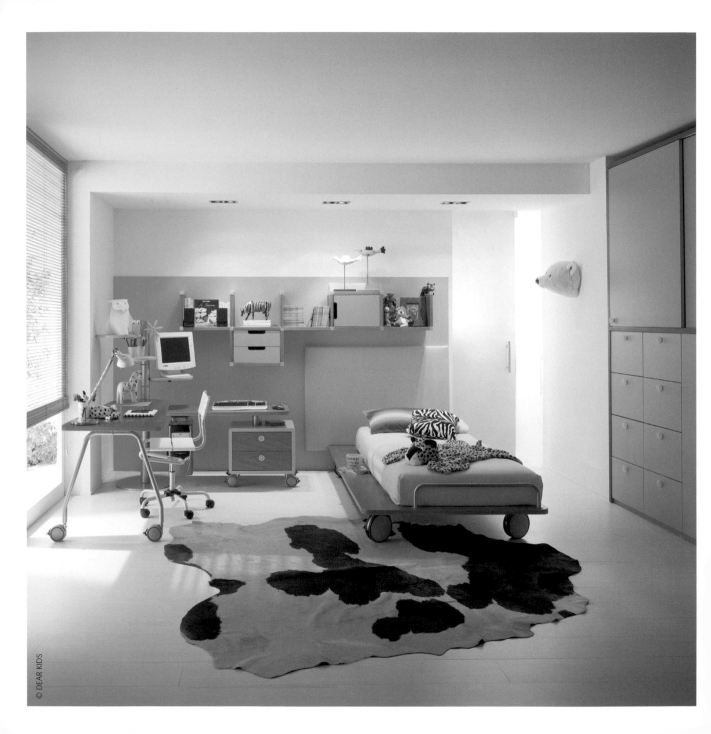

135

A raised bed, which can be placed above a storage unit or a homework desk, might be worth getting if your child has outgrown his or her bedroom.

© KINDERRÄUME

136

Creativity should play a major role in the decorating of your childrens' rooms. A good idea is to discuss their favorite themes with them.

© KINDERRÄUME

© MUEBLES BENICARLÓ

© MUEBLES BENICARLÓ

137

Creative solutions that make cleaning the bedroom efficient and fun help encourage the children to tidy up and keep things in their place.

138

A comfortable corner or study area can double as a practical guest bed if your children have regular sleepovers.

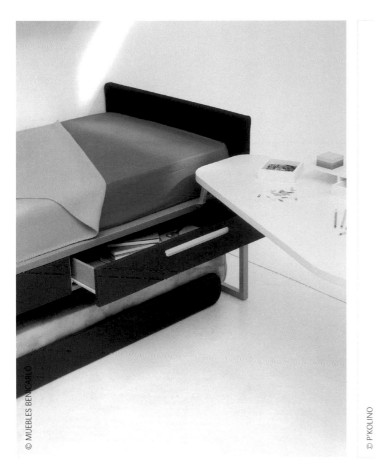

There are bunk options with clothing and toy storage incorporated for room sharing or occasional overnight sleeping.

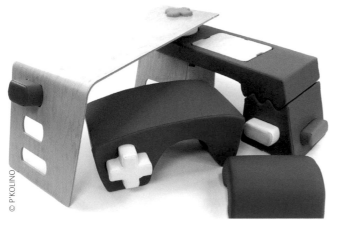

Bathrooms

While the toilets are hidden in private areas, showers and tubs can be installed in more open spaces to make the most of available views.

Filippo Bombace / © Luigi Filetici

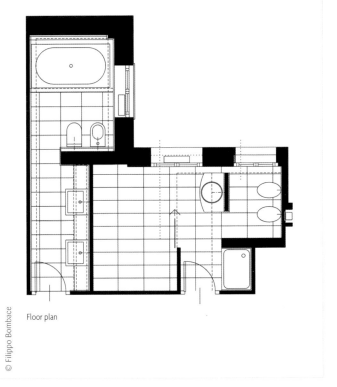

© Filippo Bombace

Floor plan

139

As an alternative to drywall and tile on your bathroom walls, natural stone conveys a soothing sensation that invites relaxation.

Carola Vannini Architecture / © Filippo Vinardi

Carola Vannini Architecture / © Filippo Vinardi

White fixtures against dark walls look sharp. While dark colors tend to make rooms look smaller, they also make them cozy and comfortable.

The technique of using Venetian plaster offers a look of antiqued wallpaper that works very well in bathrooms.

Carola Vannini Architecture / © Filippo Vinardi

Carola Vannini Architecture / © Filippo Vinardi

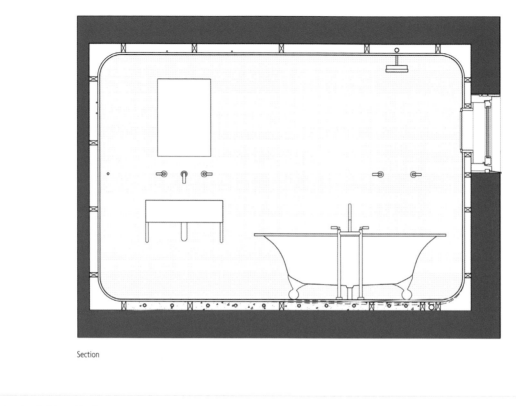

Section

Striking color and material combinations
and rounded corners stand out in this
bathroom. The ceiling, walls, and flooring
are coated in rubber.

Taking advantage of the ample space
available, this en suite bedroom and
bathroom is designed around a sculptural
vanity.

The vanity unit, which also serves as a screen, is inspired by a sheet of paper. Its design uses the fold as a countertop with a washbasin.

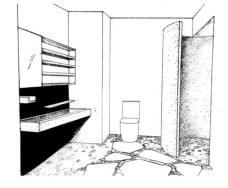

The refurbishment of this bathroom balances the existing organic forms of the space with the contemporary minimalistic fixtures.

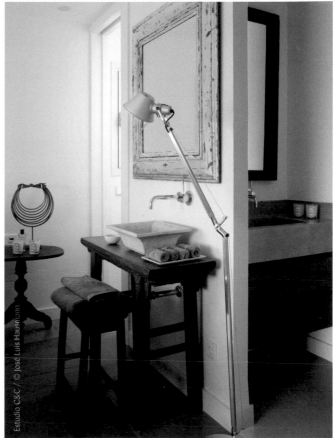

140

An old piece of furniture can find new life out of its original context to provide a personalized decor.

Material, texture, and coloration are
orchestrated to further articulate the
architectural design elements.

Many types of plinth tubs are available with air bath systems that are installed and hidden inside the plinth.

Carola Vannini Architecture / © Filippo Vinardi

Carola Vannini Architecture / © Filippo Vinardi

141

Venetian plaster creates a unique marble appearance, with subtle variations in color. The surface can be clear, coated, or burnished.

While the bathroom is enclosed in a glass container, unity with the bedroom is preserved by using the same color scheme.

Cove lighting and recessed lighting under the bathtub reinforces the architectural and design features of this en suite bedroom and bathroom.

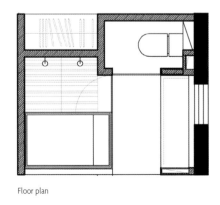

Floor plan

Mohen Design / © Mohen Design

142

A bright color scheme and glass surfaces combine to enhance the lighting effects of indirect and recessed ceiling lights.

143

Glass mosaic tiles can be quite unique and engaging. They come in solid colors and can have an iridescent finish or be slightly textured.

Filippo Bombace / © Luigi Filetici

144

For a dramatic statement, try using Venetian plaster that is tinted black, rather than just painted matte black, for some visual texture.

Despang ArchiteKten / © Olaf Baumann

Despang ArchiteKten / © Olaf Baumann

145

Small tiles provide a good grip but also require more cleaning. Use sealer or an off-white grout to minimize cleaning chores.

Wood paneling, pebble flooring, and a massive stone washbasin are key elements in this inviting and relaxing home spa.

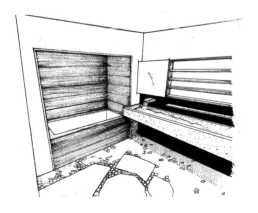

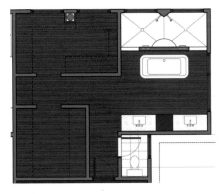

Floor plan

146

Wood paneling is suitable for bathrooms as long as there is good ventilation or a strong vent fan.

© DURAVIT

147

Combine neutral colors and rich wood finishes for an elegant and contemporary feel in the bathroom.

© TOSCOQUATTRO

148

Wall-mounted bathroom cabinets make it easy to clean the area quickly. They give the bathroom an airy feel without sacrificing storage.

© TOSCOQUATTRO

Far from being dull, monochromatic color schemes are a perfectly valid way to infuse your bathroom with a touch of elegance.

© AGAPE

Hobby a. Schuster & Maul / © Marc Hader

149

Find dark-wood accessories to calm down a bright green that you might like to use in your bathroom but haven't because you've been afraid of going overboard.

© BURGBAD20

150

A quick, easy and inexpensive way to add color to your crisp, white bathroom is to paint one wall with a vivid bright tone.

The rustic look calls for natural tones and finishes inspired by an old barn. A slightly more sophisticated air is achieved by using simpler forms.

© Pom'dOr

© Pom'dOr

Innovative designs of vanities and cabinets with high-quality finishes and hardware are a good home investment for the long term.

© Pom'dOr

Bathrooms

DIRECTORY

Aidlin Darling Design
San Francisco, CA, USA
www.aidlindarlingdesign.com

Apollo Architects & Associates
Tokyo, Japan
Seoul, South Korea
www.kurosakisatoshi.com

Archipro Architects
Tokyo, Japan
http://archiproe.jimdo.com

Barbara Appolloni, arquitecta
Barcelona, Spain
www.barbaraappolloni.com

CJ Studio
Taipei, China
www.shi-chieh-lu.com

CL3 Architects
Beijing, China
Shanghai, China
www.cl3.com

Craig Nealy Architects
New York, NY, USA
www.craignealy.com

Craig Steely Architecture
San Francisco, CA, USA
www.craigsteely.com

Dennis Gibbens Architects
Santa Monica, CA, USA
www.dga-inc.com

Desai / Chia Architecture
New York, NY, USA
www.desaichia.com

Edwards Moore
Melbourne, Australia
www.edwardsmoore.com

EOA | Elmslie Osler Architect
New York, NY, USA
www.eoarch.com

FORMA Design
Washington, DC, USA
www.formaonline.com

Gabellini Sheppard Associates
New York, NY, USA
www.gabellinisheppard.com

GRAFT Gesellschaft von Architekten
Berlin, Germany
Los Angeles, CA, USA
Beijing, China
www.graftlab.com

Guillermo Arias and Luis Cuartas
Bogotá, Colombia
www.octubre.com.co

Hofman Dujardin Architecten
Amsterdam, the Netherlands
www.hofmandujardin.nl

Hot Dog Decor
Shanghai, China
www.hotdogdecor.com

i29 | interior architects
Duivendrecht, the Netherlands
www.i29.nl

Jeff Etelemaki Design Studio
Brooklyn, NY, USA
www.je-designstudio.com

Joel Sanders Architect
New York, NY, USA
www.joelsandersarchitect.com

Joey Ho Design
Hong Kong, China
www.joeyhodesign.com

Jonathan Clark Architects
London, United Kingdom
www.jonathanclark.co.uk

KNS Architects
Mumbai, India
www.knsarchitects.com

lkmk architects
Vrilissia, Greece
www.lkmk.gr

Lakonis architekten
Vienna, Austria
www.lakonis.at

Leone Design Studio
Brooklyn, NY, USA
www.royleone.com

MACK Architect(s)
Venice, CA, USA
www.markmack.com

MESH Architectures
Brooklyn, NY, USA
http://www.mesh-arc.com

Nacho Polo Interior Designer
Miami Beach, FL, USA
www.nachopolo.com

Nest Architects
Melbourne, Australia
www.nestarchitects.com.au

Norm.Architects
Copenhagen, Denmark
www.normcph.com

Olson Kundig Architects
Seattle, WA, USA
www.olsonkundigarchitects.com

Pascal Arquitectos
Mexico D.F., Mexico
www.pascalarquitectos.com

Pepe Calderin Design
Miami, FL, USA
www.pepecalderindesign.com

PTang Studio
Hong Kong, China
www.ptangstudio.com

Simone Micheli Architectural Hero
Florence, Italy
www.simonemicheli.com

Siris / Coombs Architects
New York, NY, USA
www.siriscoombs.com

SKEW Collaborative
New York, NY, USA
Shanghai, China
Singapore, Republic of Singapore
www.sciskew.com

Ten to One
Brooklyn, NY, USA
www.tenonedesignbuild.com

Zack | de Vito Architecture
San Francisco, CA, USA
www.zackdevito.com